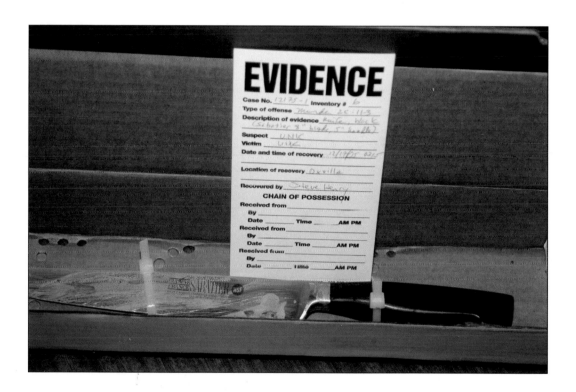

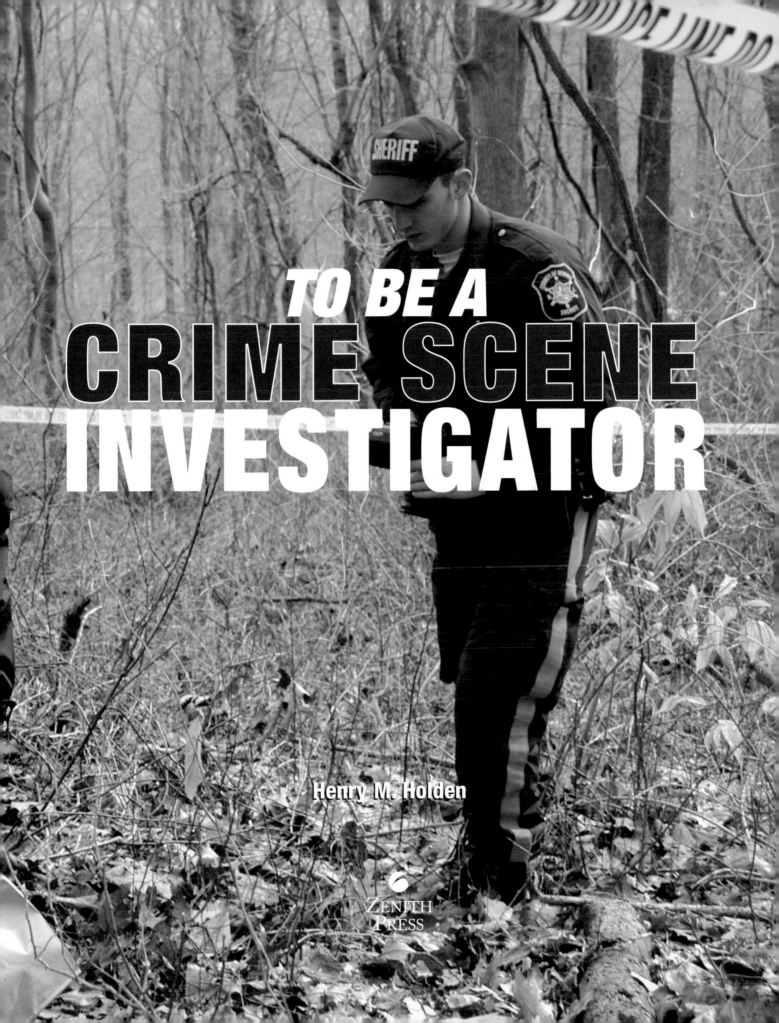

# TO BE A
# CRIME SCENE
# INVESTIGATOR

Henry M. Holden

ZENITH
PRESS

*Dedication*
To the men and women of law enforcement:
Thank you for serving, and may God bless you and keep you safe.

First published in 2006 by Zenith Press, an imprint of MBI Publishing Company, Galtier Plaza, Suite 200, 380 Jackson Street, St. Paul, MN 55101-3885 USA

MBI Publishing Company titles are also available at discounts in bulk quantity for industrial or sales-promotional use. For details write to Special Sales Manager at MBI Publishing Company, Galtier Plaza, Suite 200, 380 Jackson Street, St. Paul, MN 55101-3885 USA

ISBN-13: 978-0-7603-2524-7
ISBN-10: 0-7603-2524-3

Editors: Lindsay Hitch and Steve Gansen
Designer: Sara Grindle

Printed in China

Library of Congress Cataloging-in-Publication Data

Holden, Henry M.
  To be a crime scene investigator / Henry M. Holden.
    p. cm.
  ISBN-13: 978-0-7603-2524-7
  ISBN-10: 0-7603-2524-3
  1. Criminal investigation. 2. Criminal investigation—Vocational guidance. 3. Crime scenes. 4. Crime scene searches. I. Title.
  HV8073.H598 2006
  363.25'2--dc22

*On the cover*: In this staged photograph, it is too early for the crime scene investigators to know what happened here. All they know is that they have a victim and that a weapon is apparent, along with one cartridge case at evidence marker number three. Possibly, the victim tried to defend herself and fired one round, or perhaps the killer got off the first shot, leaving the shell casing. The medical examiner will turn the body over, examine it for gunshot wounds or other trauma, and establish the approximate time of death by inserting a temperature probe into the liver. A clean white sheet will be wrapped around the victim's corpse to preserve any evidence, and the body will be transported to the morgue for autopsy. At the morgue, additional photos and fingerprints will be taken, and the body and clothing will be examined for trace evidence. *Henry M. Holden*

*On the frontispiece*: This large kitchen knife was recovered from a homicide. A presumptive test revealed that the dried material is blood, but the lab will need to determine if it is human blood and if it belonged to the victim. The box will be sealed with the evidence sticker, and the chain of custody on the bottom of the sticker will be filled in as appropriate.

*On the title pages*: Detective Bruce Dunn gathers the bagged evidence while Detective James Rae documents the collection on digital media.

*On the back cover*:
*Top left*: This detective applies a black print powder to the side window of a vehicle.
*Bottom left*: Photographing human remains is important to demonstrate the original condition of the corpse. Close-up photos are essential because the body will continue to decay and eventually what identifying characteristics had remained will be lost. *FBI*
*Right*: This FBI special agent is training to be an evidence response team (ERT) member. She is gathering potential trace evidence with a special vacuum.

*About the Author*: Henry M. Holden is the author of fourteen adult books, including Zenith Press' *To Be A U.S. Secret Service Agent* and *To Be An FBI Special Agent*, nineteen children's books, and more than six hundred magazine articles on aviation history. In 1994, he received the New Jersey Institute of Technology Author's Award, and that same year Holden was mentioned in the Congressional Record for his works on women in aviation. Holden has been an aviation commentator for the History Channel and lives in northwestern New Jersey.

Some specific academic, physical, firearms, and defensive tactics training and evaluation procedures provided in this book are through the courtesy of Morris County Sheriff Edward V. Rochford and Director Daniel H. Colucci of the Morris County Fire Fighters and Police Training Academy. Similar training and evaluation methods are used by other agencies.

# CONTENTS

# Preface

Early crime scene investigation was a crude process: stumbling over evidence, thereby contaminating it, obtaining evidence from informers who were usually engaged in criminal activity, confessions made under duress, sticking to unreliable eyewitness accounts, or implicating innocent individuals out of revenge. It was a process that had little regard for the innocent, the victim, or for justice.

In 1829, the Metropolitan Police Act established all of London's police under the responsibility of one authority, with its headquarters at Scotland Yard. This act established the principles that shaped modern English police investigations. The first organized crime detection took place as a result of Sir Arthur Conan Doyle's novels about Sherlock Holmes. The unbelievable skill of the fictional detective to solve crimes from the smallest pieces of physical evidence inspired Scotland Yard to follow Holmes' approach at a crime scene. The British example influenced the development of criminal investigation in the United States, where large cities patterned their police efforts after the successful model in England.

The responsibility of modern law enforcement agencies is to protect the public from criminals, detect crimes, apprehend the offenders, and provide straight-forward and unequivocal evidence to judges and juries that the offenders are guilty beyond a reasonable doubt.

Criminal investigations are conducted in the United States at the municipal, state, and federal levels in accordance with established laws. The conduct of an investigation is governed by the integrity of the crime

scene investigators, physical evidence, information obtained from people, and records. Victims or witnesses still provide evidence as to when, where, how, why, and by whom the crime was committed, but it is often the forensic evidence that convicts the offender.

Modern crime scene investigation and solving crimes successfully requires a variety of methods, including crime reconstruction; collecting, preserving, and maintaining the all-important chain of custody of physical evidence; and interrogating suspects and interviewing witnesses. This is not a haphazard process but a precise, thoughtful, and scientific approach. The men and women who do this work, the crime scene investigators, are highly skilled and trained law enforcement personnel who build up years of experience both on the job and through in-service and external academic training. In *To Be a Crime Scene Investigator*, I have attempted, through the advice and counsel of those in the field, to present the information necessary to those interested in a career as a crime scene investigator.

# Acknowledgments

Morris County New Jersey's Criminal Investigation Section: front row (left to right), Detective Kelley Shanaphy, Detective Charlie Marotta, Detective Laura Valente; middle row (left to right), Detective Bruce Dunn, Detective Ed Crooker, Detective James Rae, Detective Al Dekler; top row (left to right), Detective Corporal Bill Stitt, Detective Sergeant Ed Williams, and Detective Mike Puzio. Absent from the photo are Detectives Lisa Bonfiglio and Tom Riedinger. *Morris County Sheriff's Office*

This work is the result of a collaborative effort on the part of many. It would not have been possible without the input and trust of these individuals. They come from many disciplines and all are professionals in every sense of the word. From the Morris County Fire Fighters and Police Training Academy: Chief Daniel H. Colucci, academy director, and Chief Ronald Graziano provided valuable insights and access to their academic and physical training facilities. From various county police agencies, some of the officers who volunteered as instructors at the academy are: Patrolman Samuel Trimble, Detective John Ambrose, Sergeant Don Smith, Sergeant Paul Carifi Jr., Lieutenant James Monaghan, Patrolman Robert Oranchak, Corporal Mike Lowe, Officer D. Wyatt, Patrolman John Hurd, Sheriff's Officer Steve Carro, and Agent Bill Tsigaras and Detective Mark Castellano from the Morris County prosecutor's office, and others.

My appreciation and thanks to Sheriff Edward V. Rochford, for without allowing access to his organization and to the men and women of his Criminal Investigation Section, this book would not have been possible. I have made every effort to fulfill his trust that it would be an accurate account of the work his crime scene investigators perform on a daily basis. Detective Sergeant Edward Williams gave me complete cooperation in every aspect of this project. He permitted me to sit in on a week-long crime scene investigator's class, offered ride-alongs to crime scenes, and provided access to photo records and their laboratory. His detective team of crime scene investigators who follow were all warm, welcoming, helpful, and professional, and they were especially patient to my many elementary questions. I have developed a deep respect for the work they do and the integrity they bring to the job. My thanks to: Detective Corporal Bill Stitt, Detective Lisa Bonfiglio, Detective Ed Crooker, Detective Al Dekler, Detective Bruce Dunn, Detective Mike Puzio, Detective James Rae, Detective Tom Riedinger, Detective Kelley Shanaphy, and Detective Laura Valente; to Gary Colburn of the photo unit; and my special thanks to Ginny Walsh, also

of the photo unit, who went beyond her job description in one critical aspect of this book.

From the FBI Laboratory, my special thanks to Supervisory Special Agent (SSA) Ann Todd, a friend and lifeline for this project at the FBI Laboratory; SSA Virginia Sanchez and SSA Dayna Sepeck for their efforts in the photo area; SSA Gerry Downes for his amazing insights and knowledge of behavioral science; to Chief of the Explosives Unit, Greg Carl, for his fascinating insights into bomb scene forensics; and to Special Agent Angela Bell from Headquarters. You were all helpful beyond my expectations.

My thanks and appreciation to my editor, Steve Gansen, who asked me if I would like to do this book—Steve, this was an eyeopener, and I am grateful for the opportunity—and Lindsay Hitch, also my editor on this project. Both were always professional and always helpful during the course of this project. It was a pleasure to work with both of you.

And of course, my thanks to my wife, Nancy, who was by my side throughout this project and brought to it a keen eye for which photographs worked and which did not.

To the many other people unnamed who contributed to this work, in large and small ways, I am appreciative of all your efforts.

# ONE

All law enforcement agencies provide self-defense training tactics. Immediate control of the suspect is paramount to the safety of the officer and suspect, and to a successful arrest. *FBI*

# Police Officer—
# Application and
# Training

Morris County Fire Fighters and Police Training
Academy logo

Law enforcement agencies usually require the prospective crime scene investigator (CSI) to be a sworn officer (with arrest powers and authority to carry a weapon) and serve a minimum of three to five years on the job as a criminal investigator before applying to become a crime scene investigator. There are exceptions. For example, the individual may hold a PhD in a forensic science and be an instructor at a local university, a consultant under contract on a case-by-case basis, or a qualified civilian.

In areas with large populations and high rates of violent crime, the evidence documentation and collection portion of a crime scene response may be a full-time job. Many larger police agencies have budgets for such personnel specialties.

Smaller police agencies often do not have full-time crime scene investigators. These rural agencies may have two- to three-dozen sworn officers, and about one-third of those officers are supervisory or management. Often, the crime scene investigator is a collateral job. In some jurisdictions, the local police may call upon the county sheriff's department or state police, who maintain a pool of full-time crime scene investigators.

Most police agencies require some type of two- or four-year college degree for their sworn officers. Regardless of whether the individual's education is in the social sciences, general studies, history, or criminal justice, if the individual is seeking a career as a crime scene investigator, he or she should supplement degree work with courses in computer science, forensic sciences, and photography. Some agencies may look for candidates who speak both English and a second language. A second language generally makes an individual more marketable. Many agencies also give military veterans a preference.

## APPLICATION

An information sheet, or briefing guide, about the police testing procedure is generally given to all applicants when they apply to their jurisdiction. A background investigator will usually provide the application, initial interview, and an information packet containing a job description, salary guide, list of benefits, and career paths available within the department. The background investigator will review this material, answer any questions, set a time and date for the return of the completed formal application, and schedule the testing. The investigator will also verify the applicant's identity and possession of a valid driver's license, and will arrange for the submission of fingerprints and a photo for a criminal records check. Applicants usually submit a headshot and full-body photograph for their personnel file.

"We had one applicant submit a photo of himself in a tank top, shorts, and sandals," one senior officer said. "We wonder sometimes where a person's head is when they do this, or when someone comes into an important interview in casual clothing. The information on this applicant's sheet looked solid, so I explained to him that the photo becomes part of his permanent record, should he be hired. He came back the next day with an appropriate photo and dressed in a suit and tie. He said he did not own a suit and went out and bought one just for the interview. At this point, we knew we had someone highly motivated for the job."

Stretching exercises are necessary to perform the sit and reach test. This is a measure of the flexibility of the lower back and upper leg area. It is an important area for performing police work involving a wide range of motion. The sit and reach test involves stretching out to touch the toes or beyond with extended arms from the sitting position. The score is in the inches reached on a yardstick.

Hydration in all physical exercise is important to performing well. A recruit class takes a few minutes to get hydrated during morning physical training.

As uncomfortable as they may be, warm-up stretching exercises are necessary to prevent injuries during a workout.

Part of the physical evaluation is counting the number of rungs a recruit is able to cross on the horizontal ladder in a two-minute period. The exercise involves crossing the ladder and running up and down the length of the gym several times, crossing the ladder again, and repeating the process for two minutes.

## GENERAL REQUIREMENTS TO BECOME A POLICE OFFICER

The police officer hiring process varies throughout the United States but generally takes one of three routes: civil service; non-civil service, which is sometimes called the "chief's test"; and the "Alternate Route Basic Course for Police Officers."

Competitive state and local government civil service examinations provide a way to ensure that appointments to municipal public service jobs are on merit. The chief's test, also based on merit, is a competitive test given by a local police agency. The Alternate Route Basic Course offers individuals the opportunity to attend a police training academy at their own expense, prior to being hired by a local police department. In five counties in northern New Jersey, this twenty-two-week course costs approximately $3,000 and is administered by the Morris County Fire Fighters and Police Training Academy (MCFFPTA). The law allows no more than 50 percent of a class to be composed of these individuals, and generally, about 20 to 30 percent of a recruit class is made up of these individuals. During and upon completion of academy training, the local police agencies review the graduates and generally make job offers.

While specific eligibility requirements may vary between agencies, some common requirements are:

Applicants must be U.S. citizens and at least eighteen (or twenty-one) years of age on or before the day of hire, but no older than thirty-five.

Applicants must have successfully completed a minimum of:

    a. Sixty college credits with a 2.0 grade point average from an accredited college or university, or

    b. At least two years of full-time, active military service in the U.S. military with an honorable discharge, and have a high school diploma or its equivalent.

Applicants may need to reside within a designated geographic area.

Applicants must possess a valid driver's license.

Applicants may have to pay for a part of the investigation process, such as a fee for fingerprinting.

Applicants must be of good moral character and must not be convicted of any criminal offense.

Applicants must meet minimum medical standards, as prescribed by the jurisdiction; possess visual acuity not exceeding 20/100 uncorrected, corrected to 20/30 or better with corrective lenses; be able to distinguish between the colors red, green, and yellow; and have weight in proportion to height.

Applicants successfully completing a background investigation will be given a psychological evaluation to determine suitability, and compatibility, to perform basic police functions.

As a condition of employment, applicants will be required to undergo drug screening. Positive drug tests for law enforcement results in a permanent ban from law enforcement.

All males from the ages of eighteen through twenty-five are required to register with the Federal Selective Service System under the Military Service Act and provide proof of registration. Registration with the Federal Selective Service System is usually a condition of continued employment.

## DISQUALIFICATION

There are specific issues that will automatically disqualify an applicant from consideration for a police officer position. They are: conviction of a felony offense, any repeated convictions of an offense that indicates a disrespect for the law, a lack of good moral character or disposition toward violence, discharge from employment where such discharge indicates poor behavior and/or an inability adjusting to discipline, a dishonorable discharge from the armed forces, conviction of any domestic violence offense, and failure of the

medical, physical, written psychological, oral psychological, or polygraph examination.

## TEST PREPARATION AND STUDY SUGGESTIONS

The police officer exam is not one on which a high score can be achieved by cramming the night before. Disciplined study habits, however, can lead to higher scores. Be rested before the study period. If you are tired, it will slow the learning process. If possible, schedule regular study times of a minimum thirty minutes daily. One to two hours daily is a more realistic basic goal. Distractions such as television, telephones, and children will slow learning. Find a quiet spot in the house, or go to a library. Have a comfortable desk, chair, and adequate lighting. Avoid coffee and other stimulants.

There are numerous police officer test workbooks available online and in bookstores. In general, they follow a boilerplate approach in that the same test areas are covered. The specific questions may be different, so it may be wise to purchase more than one workbook to become exposed to a larger variety of questions.

## WRITTEN EXAM

The first step in the police officer selection process after the basic interview and application is a written examination. The exams are timed, and the entire test process may last several hours. The police officer examinations are competitive, and the minimum acceptable score usually ranges from 70 to 80 percent; however, only the top-scoring individuals are selected.

Another evaluation is the number of squat thrusts performed in 90 seconds.

Detective Jack Ambrose inspects a recruit while Corporal Mike Lowe looks on, prepared to make any notes on the inspection for the recruit's record.

Sergeant Paul Carifi Jr. instructs a recruit standing at attention in a finer point of the workout. Military discipline is maintained throughout the twenty-two-week training period.

Pushups measure upper body strength; thirty to seventy-five in a minute is the goal. The more the recruit performs, the more competitive the recruit becomes in the class standing.

Stretching before the sit-up test is important. The test is a measure of the endurance of the abdominal muscles. This is an important area for satisfactory police work that may involve the use of force, and for minimizing lower back injuries. The competitive score is the number of bent-leg sit-ups performed in one minute.

Some agencies use the National Criminal Justice Officer Selection Inventory (NCJOSI). The NCJOSI is a series of multiple-choice questions designed to test job-related cognitive abilities and personality attributes necessary for the effective performance of police work. Questions on this test do not require the applicant to be familiar with police procedures but provide enough information so the answer may be based on common sense. In general, the written exam is broken down into five areas: problem solving, reading comprehension, mathematics, writing ability, and psychological/personality screening. The total time allowed for this test is one and one-half hours.

### Problem Solving

Problem solving is the ability to deal effectively with routine or unusual situations, anticipate situations, and create alternate plans of action for these situations.

On this test, there is a problem embedded in each question. The problem must be identified first, and the solution lies within the choices provided. This part of the test is difficult to study for since common sense is not something learned from a study guide.

One question may be: You see an exchange of drugs and money between two individuals on your foot patrol. The individuals see you, and each runs in a different direction. Do you:

Fire a warning shot and order them to stop?

Write down their descriptions and issue a warrant for their arrest?

Go after the suspect with the drugs?

Go after the suspect with the money?

Go after the slowest suspect?

Answer: Going after the suspect carrying the drugs is the best choice. Firing a warning shot is dangerous to innocent persons. Writing down descriptions is okay, but it allows the person with the drugs to get away. Possession of money is not a crime, and going after the slowest suspect, if he is not carrying the drugs, is futile.

### Reading Comprehension

Reading comprehension is the ability to understand written materials. Police officers must study and interpret large amounts of information and data. They must read and understand laws, procedures, and correspondence. The best way to improve reading comprehension is to read often, and read materials that interest you. Fiction, nonfiction, newspapers, and magazine articles are good sources. Try to understand what the author is trying to say. Is there an underlying meaning in the piece? Are there ideas that support any conclusions? If so, which ones are important, and can they be prioritized? Employing this technique in all your reading will improve your overall reading comprehension. Another way to improve reading comprehension is to improve your vocabulary. Set a goal of learning and using a certain number of new words each week. The more words you know and understand, the more you will understand what you are reading.

### Mathematics

Mathematics plays an important role in police work and crime scene investigations. Mathematics treats exact relations existing between quantities in such a way that other quantities may be deduced from them. Some of the uses of mathematics in police work may include measuring the diameter of a crime scene to determine its perimeter and estimating distances traveled.

The mathematics exam generally deals with fractions, decimals, percentages, ratios, and proportions. In this area, there are study guides available, and the police officer test study guides usually include sections on mathematics.

### Writing Ability

Writing ability is the correct use of grammar, spelling, punctuation, and vocabulary when reducing interviews or other information accurately to a written format that is organized in a logical manner. Report writing is something a police officer will do throughout his or her career, and it is a critical skill. The applicant will not write a police report, but instead, the questions in this section may take one of several forms. The first may be reading a narrative. A blank report form may be the answer sheet, and the applicant will be asked to find specific information in the narrative and fill it in on the report.

A second format may be a completed report. The questions will refer to the report, and the answers are imbedded in the report. There may be several facts about the crime scene that are part of the report, so it is important to recognize the correct who, what, when, where, and why, as there may be more than one of each of these in the report.

Grammar, vocabulary, and spelling play an important role in a police officer's ability to communicate effectively. If the information in a police report is vague, incorrect, seriously misspelled, or grammatically incorrect, it detracts from the competence of the officer (and the agency) and may ultimately hinder the successful prosecution of an offender. There are study guides and books available on basic grammar, online, and in bookstores. In addition, most word processing programs have grammar-checking features, which will identify incorrect grammar usage and help an applicant improve his or her grammar.

Spelling questions may make up 5 to 10 percent of the exam. Again, there are spelling guides available commercially to assist those who may need to brush up on this skill. Improving vocabulary by learning new words will also aid in improving one's spelling accuracy.

A former marine, Patrolman Samuel Trimble serves as a recruit drill instructor and knows the nuances of inspection and drill. He has some recruits sweating the answers.

Detective Jack Ambrose listens to a response from a recruit during inspection. Corporal Mike Lowe looks on.

Close-order drill is an integral part of police recruit training.

Patrolman Samuel Trimble adjusts a recruit's tie, while Patrolman Robert Oranchak takes notes. All instructors at the MCFFPTA are volunteers from local police departments and released by their agencies for this duty.

After an hour of physical training, the recruits have about nine minutes to shower and fall out for inspection. The rows must be perfectly straight for the inspecting officer. Recent classes have had a large number of ex-military members as recruits, and they fall into the quasi-military routine much faster than civilian recruits, according to the instructors. "You can tell who the ex-military people are," said one instructor. "The light comes on much sooner."

## Psychological/Personality Screening

The psychological test is a two-part exam, written and oral. Virtually all law enforcement agencies require a psychological or personality pre-employment screening of candidates. Historically, psychological and personality screening has been a way to cull out the unstable individuals with obvious mental illnesses that would make them a clear and present danger to the public's safety because of their access to firearms.

Individuals with suicidal or homicidal tendencies, or those whose grasp of reality is erratic, are obvious candidates for rejection. However, with the increasing professionalism of law enforcement, including increased educational requirements and more careful and comprehensive background investigation methods, such individuals rarely make it through the process.

### PERSONAL BACKGROUND TEST

Some police agencies give their applicants a personal background test using the Law Enforcement Candidate Record (LECR) exam, which provides multiple-choice questions. This test gives the agency some data on the type of individual the applicant is, from the books he or she reads to the number and types of friends the applicant has, and how often they interact. This test produces a statistical comparison for possible matchup to successful police officers. There are 185 questions, and the test usually takes two to four hours.

The written questions may range from personal feelings to moral judgments. There is generally no right or wrong answer. For example: You are passed over for a promotion, how do you feel?

A. better,

B. despair,

C. happy for the other person,

D. determined to try again.

Or: A person you know takes some copy paper home from the office. Is it:

A. employee theft,

B. a trivial matter,

C. acceptable behavior,

D. okay if it happens only once or twice?

Your impulse on question two may be to say "A" is correct since you are applying for a law enforcement position. That answer is correct only if you truly feel that way, and it reflects your overall attitude. It is critical to answer questions on this test from your belief system and not to respond with the answer you think the testers are looking for.

Only the top percentage of the most competitive individuals taking the written examination will be eligible to participate in the next steps of the hiring process. Being on an eligible list, however, does not imply or guarantee an offer of employment.

## BACKGROUND INVESTIGATION

The rigorous background investigation will verify previous employment, education, credit history, law enforcement contacts, reference checks, and interviews with friends, family, employers, and neighbors. The investigation will also look at the number of jobs the applicant has held. Agencies generally prefer applicants with life experience that can be examined. Too many jobs, however, may be an indicator of instability, a lack of maturity, or unresolved authority issues.

In conducting the background interviews, investigators place emphasis on several areas: character, associates, and

Every morning, after close-order drill, recruits turn out for morning Colors.

In the early phases of training, the recruits are allowed to help their buddies. Later, however, they must perform as many pull-ups as possible without any assistance. The pull-ups are not timed, and peer pressure will weigh heavily in each person's performance. The number of pull-ups they do will be ranked and put into an equation that will give them a standing within the class.

reputation, to name a few. "We look into their past behavior," said one senior officer, "because past behavior is a good predictor of future behavior."

## INTERVIEW

After the successful completion of the background investigation, the psychological test, and credit history check, the applicant is required to appear before a panel of senior officers for a formal interview. At this time, the panel will measure the applicant's responses to a series of subjective questions related to the position to which he or she is applying. Information gleaned from the applicant's application and background check will be used during the interview.

There is no way to prepare for this interview since the applicant has no prior knowledge of the questions or the topics covered. There are things the applicant can do, however, that may lead to a more positive outcome. For the initial and subsequent formal interview, show respect for the process by dressing conservatively; have a clean-cut appearance, and choose an outfit carefully. Men should wear a well-pressed business suit, a long-sleeved shirt with an interesting (but not gaudy) tie, and well-shined shoes. Women should choose business attire and avoid perfumes and colognes. Men should avoid aftershave lotion. Nervousness will cause perspiration, so an unscented antiperspirant is advised. It is not helpful to offend an interviewer who may be sensitive or allergic to certain scents. Men should avoid jewelry other than a watch or wedding band. A woman should choose jewelry that complements her outfit, is not distracting, and does not make a statement.

This interview is a major decision point in the process. Check the route to the interview location beforehand, and if possible, travel it on a dry run. You should arrive early. This demonstrates that you have planned for possible road or transit delays, and that you respect the other person's time. It also gives you a chance to prepare mentally.

The interview panel is looking for maturity, common sense, good judgment, compassion, integrity, honesty, and reliability in all your responses. Remember, one of the panel member's roles may be to get under your skin, to upset you, or to get you angry or confused. It is part of the test. If you respond in an angry or confused way during the interview, the panel will wonder how well you will respond to pressure on the job.

"Competitive state and local governments' civil service examinations provide a way to ensure that appointments to municipal public service jobs are on merit," said Chief Daniel H. Colucci, the Morris County Police Training Academy director. "After the successful completion of the background investigation, the psychological test, and the credit history check, the applicant is required to appear before a panel comprised of senior officers for a formal interview. Different panels will look for different things. I often ask, 'What is the most difficult thing in life you've had to deal with? How did you deal with it?' We look at the personality throughout the process, and how successfully he or she dealt with past problems confronting them."

"During the interview, you will be walking a fine line," said academy police coordinator, Chief Ronald Graziano. "You must present a self-confident, poised, and polite persona, yet not arrogant. Be yourself, and not the person you think we want. Communicate clearly in all your responses. As a police officer, you will be communicating with the community, and we will be looking for how well you do it now."

## PHYSICAL FITNESS

A physical test is usually given to applicants prior to entering a police academy to determine if the individual meets the minimum standards. These fitness entrance requirements help to ensure that each recruit can undergo the physical demands of an academy without undue risk of injury and with a level of fatigue tolerance adequate to meet all training requirements.

As a law enforcement officer, it is in your best interest, and that of fellow officers, to be as fit as possible. In order to pass the physical entrance requirements for the academy and completion of the course, the applicant must be in good physical condition. "Recruits usually have three to four months' notification before classes begin," said one senior officer. "That is enough time to begin a progressive physical conditioning program in advance of academic training."

There are three main components of physical training: flexibility training, aerobic training, and strength training. The guidelines for these can be organized under the acronym FITT, which stands for frequency, intensity, time, and type.

Flexibility pertains to the range of motion of the joints and muscles. Lack of lower back flexibility is a major risk factor for an injury in a suspect restraint. There are two main types of stretching exercises to improve flexibility: static and ballistic. Frequency refers to stretching movements on a regular basis. Of the three components of physical training, intensity requires the least effort. The intensity of any stretching exercise should be pain free. Most experts recommend about thirty to sixty seconds per stretch. Most stretching routines can be completed in ten to fifteen minutes per session.

The Illinois Law Enforcement Training and Standards Board recognized the importance of physical fitness for police academy performance (and eventual job performance) and established the Peace Officer Wellness Evaluation Report (POWER) test for entering any of the Illinois-certified police academies. Tests similar to this one are used in other agencies. The Illinois POWER test consists of four basic tests: sit and reach, sit-ups, bench press, and 1.5-mile run. The applicant will be required to provide medical clearance from a physician prior to participation in this assessment.

Police recruits are given a daily workout. In the early phase of police training, those recruits who have not developed endurance before arriving for training will drop out early. Later, they will run the 1.5-mile run, a timed run to measure the heart and vascular system's capability to transport oxygen.

Physical training takes place in any weather. This class began in August 2005, when temperatures were hovering around 100 degrees, and ended in December when temperatures were below freezing. "Some of the recruits had to learn how to hydrate themselves quickly," said one instructor. Some of the recruits were out of shape when they reported for training and dropped out when they could not keep up.

In the early weeks of physical training, the unprepared recruits have difficulty with the wall jump and other strenuous exercises. New recruits either arrive in shape or get in shape quickly, or they do not survive the training. Often, they remove themselves voluntarily from the program.

The purpose of aerobic or cardiovascular training is to improve the heart and vascular system's capacity to transport oxygen. It is a key way to maintain an acceptable percentage of body fat, to become less likely to surrender to fatigue, and to decrease future heart disease. The American College of Sports Medicine recommends a frequency of aerobic training of three to five times a week. The intensity of aerobic training should be at a training-zone level of 60 to 90 percent of your age-predicted maximum heart rate.

| TYPICAL FITNESS TEST | | | |
| --- | --- | --- | --- |
| **MALE** | | | |
| **AGE** | **20-29** | **30-39** | **40-49** |
| Sit and Reach | 16.0 | 15.0 | 13.8 |
| 1-Minute Situp | 37 | 34 | 28 |
| 1.5-Mile Run (minutes) | 13.4 | 14.3 | 15.2 |
| | | | |
| **FEMALE** | | | |
| **AGE** | **20-29** | **30-39** | **40-49** |
| Sit and Reach | 18.8 | 17.8 | 16.8 |
| 1-Minute Situp | 31 | 24 | 19 |
| 1.5-Mile Run (minutes) | 16.2 | 16.5 | 17.5 |

To calculate age-predicted maximum heart rate, subtract age from 220. For a 25-year-old officer that would be 25-220 = 195 beats per minute. For the training zone, multiply age-predicted maximum by 0.60 and 0.90 = 117–175 beats per minute.

Recruits warm up with various aerobic exercises. Here they skip rope for approximately five minutes. They will get a short break for hydration and begin their morning exercise routine. *FBI*

The purpose of strength training is to increase muscle mass, decrease body fat, and improve the functional ability of the musculoskeletal system. Upper body strength and abdominal strength are important areas in that low strength levels have a bearing on upper torso and lower back disorders, as well as the ability to successfully restrain suspects. In establishing a schedule of strength training, you should recognize that a body requires about forty-eight hours to recover from previous strength training. This means that the best

Instructor Dereck Wyatt of the Livingston, New Jersey, Police Department is inspecting the recruits as they take a breather. The agility run, one of the physical measurements that is not timed, is conducted indoors. A recruit runs through a 1.5-mile course that determines his or her ability to stop, change direction, and run around obstacles. Participants are given two attempts with the better of the two scored. Each test is compared to age and gender norms.

program would be one of two to three times a week on nonconsecutive days. The force exerted should be challenging without producing fatigue by either increasing the number of repetitions with the same weight, or increasing the weight with the same number of repetitions. Forty-five to sixty minutes should be adequate for a routine that does not induce fatigue. The type of workout should include all major muscle groups: hips, legs, torso, and midsection.

### THE STANDARDS
The actual performance requirement for each test is based upon norms for a national population sample. The applicant must pass every test, and the required performance to pass each test is based upon age (by decade) and gender. While the absolute performance is different for each category, the relative level of effort is identical for each age and gender group. All applicants are required to meet the same percentile range of their respective age and gender group.

### ACADEMICS
While academy training varies from one agency to another, the MCFFPTA is a typical example, with a twenty-two-week (990-hour) curriculum running Monday

Morris County Fire Fighters and Police Training Academy academic topics include human behavior, criminal law, traffic law and enforcement, report writing, motor vehicle stops, vehicle operations, weapons of mass destruction, chemical agent devices, youth gang awareness, criminal investigation procedures, and more.

through Friday from 7:00 a.m. to 5:00 p.m. "It is not a residency course, and I sometimes think it's more stressful this way than a live-in course," said one instructor. "Here, the recruit goes home each night to deal with family issues as well as studying for the next day. One recruit's wife had a baby while he was in training. That has to be extra stressful."

The curriculum includes classroom instruction in constitutional law, civil rights, state laws, local ordinances, and accident investigation. Recruits also receive training and supervised experience in patrol, traffic control, and use of firearms, self-defense, first aid, and emergency response.

The evaluation of trainees is on a regular basis at the police academy with weekly academic and physical training exams, one week of firearms training and evaluation, defensive tactics evaluation, and practical applications of this training at the end of the training period.

### DRUG TESTING
Trainees will be required to submit one or more urine specimens for drug testing while they attend a mandatory basic training course. All drug testing conducted during mandatory basic training will comply with rules

Trainees also learn how to handle a police vehicle in various conditions, from high-speed chases to sharp turns on slick surfaces. *FBI*

and regulations established by the agency's training standards. Individual trainees may also be required to submit a urine specimen for testing when there is reasonable suspicion that the trainee is illegally using drugs. A trainee may be ordered to submit to a drug test based on reasonable suspicion only with the approval of the county prosecutor, the chief executive officer of the trainee's agency, or the academy director.

## FIREARMS AND DEFENSIVE TRAINING

Police officers must be intimately familiar with firearms and able to restrain aggressive suspects. During firearms training week, recruits will fire 1,500 rounds,

A small sample of the thousands of rounds fired in training police officers to shoot well.

Detective Lisa Bonfiglio, a crime scene investigator with the Morris County criminal investigation section, completes the inspection of a recruit's handgun prior to a practice round of shooting the basic pistol course.

During firearms training, recruits will fire the full course in practice eight times and fire about fifteen hundred rounds in a week. The course consists of sixty rounds of handgun qualification fired three times with an average score of 80 percent, or forty-eight hits in the target area. They also fire forty rounds of night handgun qualification and twenty rounds of shotgun familiarization. They will fire from the 25-, 15-, 10-, 7-, 5-, and 1-yard lines. They will fire standing, kneeling, strong hand, support hand, from behind cover, and in the open. The 1-yard range assumes the officer is in an interview position, and he (or she) will hold the weapon close to his body while placing his support hand near his shirt top. This should prevent the suspect from grabbing the weapon or from pulling the officer into him.

Deputy Chief Ed Facas is the range master. The monitor in front of him allows him to see the active targets, and the mouse will move the targets to prepositioned spots on the range. The device to his right is part of a two-way communications system between him and the instructors on the range.

Sergeant Tom Stoner of the East Hanover, New Jersey, Police Department volunteers to teach recruits shooting skills. Stoner instructs a recruit on the proper loading of the Remington 870 shotgun. The shell fired contains nine pellets each approximately the size of a .32-caliber round. For each foot the rounds travel, they spread out one inch, so the weapon is not very effective beyond twenty to twenty-five yards.

> When an officer shoots a subject, it is done with the explicit intention of immediately incapacitating that subject in order to stop whatever threat to life or physical safety is posed by the subject. Immediate incapacitation is defined as the sudden physical or mental inability to pose any further risk or injury to others.

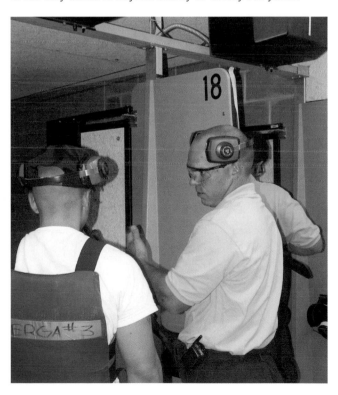

Recruits here are being given one-on-one shotgun training from firearms instructors. The instructor on the left is Mark Mekita of the Morris County Park Police.

Instructor Charles Cunningham of the Morris County prosecutor's office is explaining a point to a recruit. Ear and eye protection is a must on the firing range.

Most law enforcement officers must qualify twice a year on their handguns and shotguns, both in daylight and nighttime conditions. Sheriff's Officer Gary Schue is reviewing a perfect score shot by Lieutenant Paul Carifi Sr. Pistol training is oriented toward center-of-mass shooting as illustrated in the target. Proper shot placement is a hit in the center of that part of the adversary.

practicing various shooting techniques and skills. The full course is practiced eight times in preparation for the testing phase of the course, which is the successful firing of the handgun qualification course. The course consists of sixty rounds of handgun qualification, fired three times with an average score of 80 percent; forty rounds of night handgun qualification, also with a score of 80 percent; and twenty rounds of shotgun familiarization.

## WORKING CONDITIONS

Successful applicants hired as police officers begin their careers as probationary police officers (PPOs). Each PPO must complete a twelve- to eighteen-month probationary period, during which there are field evaluations of his or her performance on a regular basis.

Uniformed officers and detectives are usually scheduled to work a five-day, 40-hour week, with some Saturday or Sunday work, plus paid overtime. Shift work is necessary because protection must be provided around the clock.

Some of the physical and environmental conditions that police officers experience are: detecting odors, such as those caused by smoke or gas leaks; working outdoors

in all weather conditions; walking and/or standing in an assigned area; and driving or sitting in a patrol car while remaining alert.

The job is also physically demanding at times: running after a fleeing suspect; climbing or running up stairs; carrying an injured adult; physically restraining persons to prevent escape; and engaging in hand-to-hand struggles.

Understanding verbal communications over the radio with background noise, reading and writing under low-light conditions, carrying or wearing heavy equipment, and wearing soft body armor are also challenges of the job.

A task analysis study conducted by the New Jersey Division of Criminal Justice Police Training Commission revealed that a police officer may be called upon to perform over six hundred individual mental or physical tasks.

Police academy training is similar to a military boot camp. Drill instructor Sergeant Don Smith of the Randolph, New Jersey, Police Department dresses down a recruit who left a piece of lint on his uniform. The recruit on the left is the individual's partner and as such is held equally responsible.

All recruits undergo various defensive tactics training. Recruits practice a martial arts kick. This training will be part of later practical training exercises.

Sheriff's Officer Steve Carro, one of the volunteer instructors, demonstrates a martial arts punch.

"Pain, without injury, works wonders when trying to subdue a suspect," said Lieutenant James Monaghan. He demonstrates the pressure point on a recruit.

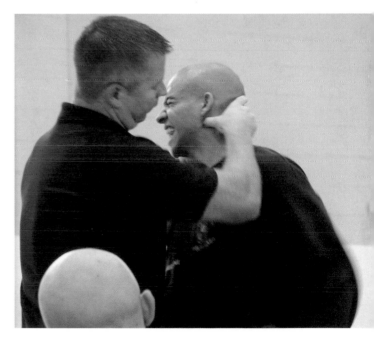

Lieutenant Monaghan applies his left hand to the right side of the recruit's face and applies pressure to a point just behind the jawbone. At this point, the recruit volunteer can think of nothing but the pain in his jaw. He becomes instantly compliant and can be restrained without injury to himself or the officer.

Proper use of defensive tactics often can spell the difference between a successful arrest and serious injury to the officer. During basic training, all male recruits must keep their heads shaved. Females must wear their hair short or pinned up.

Sheriff's Officer Steve Carro's hand waits to absorb a punch from a recruit.

Two recruits are practicing a traffic stop. A traffic stop can be a dangerous situation. The officer does not know if the occupants are armed and dangerous or just citizens who forgot to renew their registration. The driver of the car is instructor Ryan Hickman of the Stanhope, New Jersey, Police Department, and the passenger is Instructor Megan McCluskey of the Hopatcong Police Department. Instructor Shawn Frawley of the Denville, New Jersey, Police Department is observing the exercise.

## THE ROLE AND RESPONSIBILITIES OF FIRST RESPONDERS

The first responder to a crime scene is usually a uniformed officer. He or she faces several considerations. The first responsibility is to ensure the safety of others present. Any injured victims may need immediate attention, witnesses may want to leave the scene at the first opportunity, and the criminal activity may be ongoing.

The officer should record the exact time of his or her arrival. It is also critical that the police officers understand the need to preserve and control the crime scene by securing and defining the entire scene, noting all exits and paths of entry, isolating a perimeter with some type of barrier, identifying and securing witnesses and victims, documenting their observations, and removing others from the immediate area. Officers must determine whether any evidence is present, and controlling its condition may also be an issue.

The officer assigned to the crime scene's main entry must log in all authorized visitors, including name, stated purpose, and arrival and departure times. Absolutely no undocumented visitors should be allowed in the crime scene area.

Hickman decided to run but was apprehended moments later. The recruits are immediately debriefed and discuss what they would do differently the next time.

When the passenger distracted the recruit, Instructor Hickman pulled a gun and resisted the recruit's efforts to control him. In real life, this could have been a life-and-death situation.

In another exercise, a backup patrol unit provides cover for the arresting officers. A gun was found in the vehicle, and all the individuals will be removed from the vehicle one at a time, handcuffed, searched, and taken into custody.

Other officers will continue to cover the officer restraining the individual. Controlling the suspect immediately is critical to the safety of the officer and the suspect.

Once the individual is secured with handcuffs, a thorough search is made before the individual is placed in the patrol unit.

Some law enforcement agencies require their sworn personnel to qualify on both indoor and outdoor ranges.

Police recruits are given a demonstration of the effectiveness of soft body armor. Range Master Ed Facas fired several rounds from a 9mm pistol at 20 yards. The recruits approach the dummy to inspect the damage.

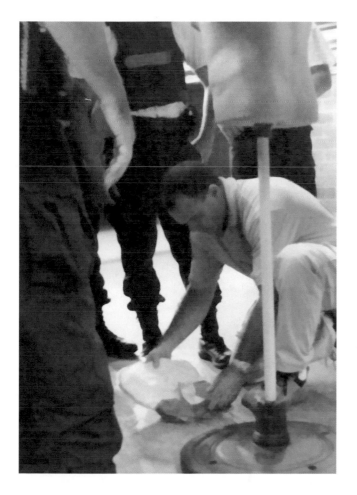

The goal of law enforcement is to safely apprehend a suspect, to present the suspect with sudden and overwhelming force that prevents aggressive action on the part of the suspect. *ICE*

**Left:** Range Master Ed Facas is digging the 9mm slugs from the vest. None of the rounds penetrated through the vest. Facas said, "The manufacturer of the body armor recommends returning the vest every five years. This vest is twenty-five years old and still doing its job. If you got them, wear them—they work," he said.

## TEN DEADLY ERRORS A POLICE OFFICER CAN MAKE:

1. Failing to maintain proficiency and care of weapon, vehicle, and equipment.
2. Improperly searching and improperly using handcuffs.
3. Being sleepy or asleep. How well can you react when you are either?
4. Relaxing too soon, usually to "phony" silent alarm calls.
5. Missing the danger signs.
6. Taking a bad position when writing a citation.
7. Failing to watch their hands. Where else can the subject hold a gun, knife, or club?
8. Displaying tombstone courage—why wait for a backup?
9. Being preoccupied with personal problems.
10. Being apathetic.

## MORRIS COUNTY FIRE FIGHTERS AND POLICE TRAINING ACADEMY CORE VALUES

1. Honesty.
2. Sense of urgency—undertake every task expediently.
3. Attention to detail—pay close attention to every part of the task.
4. Team orientation—work together for the betterment of the whole.
5. Professionalism—look sharp, speak articulately, and do not leave until the task is completed and correct.
6. Adaptability—flexible with a high degree of performance. Able to divide attention and handle several tasks simultaneously.
7. Self-discipline—the internal driver prompting an officer to do the right thing regardless of the surrounding circumstances.
8. Officer safety consciousness—maintain the high degree of situational awareness necessary to survive each day.

## LAW ENFORCEMENT CODE OF ETHICS

As a law enforcement officer, my fundamental duty is to serve mankind; to safeguard lives and property; to protect the innocent against deception, the weak against oppression or intimidation, and the peaceful against violence or disorder; and to respect the constitutional rights of all men to liberty, equality, and justice.

I will keep my private life unsullied as an example to all; maintain courageous calm in the face of danger, scorn, or ridicule; develop self-restraint; and be constantly mindful of the welfare of others. Honest in thought and deed, in both my personal and official life, I will be exemplary in obeying the laws of the land and the regulations of my department. Whatever I see or hear of a confidential nature or that is confided in me in my official capacity will be kept ever secret, unless revelation is necessary in the performance of my duty.

I will never act officiously or permit personal feelings, prejudices, animosities, or friendships to influence my decision. With no compromise for crime and with relentless prosecution of criminals, I will enforce the law courteously and appropriately without fear or favor, malice or ill will, never employing unnecessary force or violence and never accepting gratuities.

I recognize the badge of my office as a symbol of public faith, and I accept it as a public trust to be held so long as I am true to the ethics of police service. I will constantly strive to achieve these objectives and ideals, dedicating myself before God to my chosen profession . . . law enforcement.

Being assaulted or killed in the line of duty represents a reality faced by every law enforcement officer who pins on a badge. For the period from 1993 through 2002, 706 officers died in the line of duty in the United States and its territories, including seventy who died on September 11, 2001.

Every five days, an officer is murdered. In 2002, 58,066 were assaulted in the line of duty, an average of 160 every day. In 2004, 57 law enforcement officers were killed in fifty separate incidents. An examination of data from the past two, five, and ten years showed that the number of officers slain in 2004 was 5 more than the 52 killed in 2003, 6 more than the 51 slain in 2000, but 17 less than the 74 officers killed in 1995.

After several years on the job, a uniformed officer may have an opportunity to apply for a crime scene investigator's position. Many CSI personnel used their off-time as a police officer to attend college part-time and study the forensic sciences needed to be a crime scene investigator.

Police officers and detectives held about 840,000 jobs in 2002. Local governments employed about 81 percent. State police agencies employed about 11 percent, and various federal agencies employed about 6 percent.

## LEVELS OF FORCE

Police officers, sheriff's deputies, and other law enforcement officers are responsible for the protection of life and property and the enforcement of laws and regulations. This work involves an element of personal danger and frequent contact with the public under routine and emergency conditions.

Recruits at the MCFFPTA and other agencies must pass a written test on the use of force with at least an 80 percent. There are five levels of force they must understand:

The goal of level-one force is to persuade someone to do something. The means to achieve this is verbal dialogue (e.g., advice, warnings, requests, and orders). It does not involve any hands-on application.

The goal of level-two force is to achieve compliance and involves actual physical contact, including physically escorting or carrying someone from point A to point B. If an individual interferes with a crime scene and refuses an officer's orders to stay back, the officer would be justified in escalating the force to level two and physically escorting the person away from the scene.

The goals of level-three force are compliance and control using compression techniques or control devices. Compression techniques include wristlocks, arm bars, physical control holds, and the use of pressure point control tactics. Control devices consist of such tools as handcuffs, restraints, pepper spray, canines, Tasers, and stun guns. For example, an individual escorted at the force level-two stage suddenly starts resisting efforts to take him away. At that point, the escorting officer is justified in increasing the level of force to level three to get the subject to comply and to bring him under control.

The goal of level-four force is self-defense and can include personal and impact weapons. Officers frequently are assaulted, so to defend themselves and prevent or neutralize such attacks, they may resort to personal weapons (e.g., hands, fists, and feet) to hit or kick. Or, they can use impact weapons, such as batons, flashlights, and kinetic energy projectiles (e.g., shotguns that fire beanbag rounds or rubber bullets).

The goal of level-five force is to stop someone. To accomplish this, officers can employ deadly force, which includes the use of a firearm, another deadly weapon, or a roadblock. All of these forms of force are potentially lethal. If the demonstrator in level two manages to obtain a gun or knife, and attacks or is about to attack the officer, the use of deadly force would be justified.

Some agencies use color-coded handcuffs to permit transporting officers to know the difference between the average inmates and those who should be considered a greater threat.

# TWO

The FBI simulates crime scenes to train its evidence response technicians (ERTs). The area is secured with tape, a command post is established outside the scene, and each ERT has a specific assignment. Designating a command post location beyond the crime scene will ensure the exchange of information between search and investigative personnel, coordination with other law enforcement agencies, and controlled access to the scene.

# Becoming a Crime Scene Investigator

Crime scenes are where you find them, and FBI ERT trainees learn to process and package evidence in a wooded area. *FBI*

A candidate for the crime scene investigator (CSI) position must have an in-depth knowledge of police department policies and practices. The selection of a crime scene investigator is usually based upon a demonstrated knowledge of police investigative techniques, knowledge of search and seizure laws, rules for the chain of custody, and the police officer's role in criminal prosecution.

## THE CRIME SCENE TEAM

The crime scene team consists of experts from law enforcement and various forensic science disciplines. There are municipal detectives, crime scene investigators, county prosecutors and major crime (death) detectives, and a medical examiner.

Some crime scene investigators are professional, and others are specialized and technical. The following is a partial list of professional forensic specialties that may be called into a criminal investigation: anthropologist, botanist, engineer, entomologist, medical examiner, odontologist, and surveyor.

## EVIDENCE PROCEDURE

Although the procedures may vary between agencies, the key to proper crime scene investigation is always to take time to do a thorough job and document everything.

### FIRST STAGE
1. Approach the scene safely.
2. Secure and protect the scene.
3. Start an initial survey.

### SECOND STAGE
4. Photograph the area extensively.
5. Evaluate all the physical evidence and decide the order of collecting it, with trace evidence collected first.
6. Make a narrative description—written, audio, video, or all three.

### THIRD STAGE
7. Draw diagrams and sketches of the scene that put the evidence in a specific perimeter.
8. Collect the evidence. The process is delicate, time consuming, precise, and rigorous if done correctly.
9. Conduct a final survey.
10. Release the crime scene

Clinical forensic nursing is the application of clinical nursing practice to trauma survivors or crime victims, involving the identification of the unrecognized, unidentified injuries and the proper processing of the forensic evidence. A forensic nurse is a registered nurse with additional training. For example: examining evidence and assisting the medical examiner at death scene investigations, handling rape kits, recognizing as-yet-unreported crimes, domestic or child abuse examinations in an emergency room, assisting with the recovery and identification of remains at a disaster with mass casualties, and preparing medical exhibits for the courtroom.

FBI special agent emergency response team (ERT) technicians and selected support employees have forensic specialties: photographers, sketch artists, evidence collectors/processors, bomb technicians, computer specialists, engineers, surveyors, forensic anthropologists, botanists, odontologists, entomologists, medical specialists, and arson investigators, to name some. Specialized technology ERT personnel use includes thermal imaging and fiberscopes, ground-penetrating radar to locate evidence beneath the ground surface, and side-scan sonar to locate evidence underwater.

This FBI special agent is training to be an evidence response team (ERT) member. She is gathering potential trace evidence with a special vacuum. Instead of just entering a major crime scene, crime scene investigators are taught to vacuum their way in because evidence may be present at the entry point. If they vacuum after they enter, they may have contaminated the evidence. The scene is divided into sections on a grid. After vacuuming one section, the filter is removed, labeled and identified, and logged in, and a new filter is added for the next section on the grid.

During the morning coffee break, the instructors are discussing the finer points and popularity of digital photography with a new crime scene investigator.

Most technical crime scene investigator forensic positions require specific educational backgrounds. Some of these positions include computer forensic technician, clinical forensic nurse, fingerprint examiner, firearms and ballistics examiner, bloodstain examiner, and document examiner.

Depending on the agency, crime scene investigators may work on small or complex crime scene investigations, including violent crimes such as homicide, suicide, sexual assault, and armed robberies; home invasions; and property crimes such as burglaries. The CSI will try to establish what happened and will attempt to identify the responsible individual(s). The ability to recognize and properly collect physical evidence is critical to both solving and prosecuting crimes.

## CRIME SCENE INVESTIGATOR

Crime scene investigators undergo extensive training and build up considerable experience on the job. While they typically have a solid general-knowledge base, they may not be experts in every aspect of forensic science, as Hollywood would lead one to believe. Some forensic technicians may specialize in one area, such as bones, blood spatter, trace evidence, tire or tool marks, or document analysis, and they pool their expertise by working as a team.

Crime scene investigators need above-average written communication skills. They will be required to take thorough notes to complete a comprehensive

Morris County Sheriff's Criminal Investigation Section (CIS) Detective Corporal Bill Stitt (left) and Detective Mike Puzio are explaining basic crime scene photography to new crime scene investigators.

written report. They must also have exceptional verbal skills to work as a liaison between the investigators, pathologists, and prosecuting attorneys. From time to time, they may be required to give accurate or expert testimony in a court of law.

## CIVILIAN CRIME SCENE INVESTIGATORS

If, for some reason, becoming a police officer is not an option, another route to becoming a crime scene investigator is as a civilian. There are more than eighteen thousand police agencies in the United States, and some agencies employ full-time civilian crime scene investigators. To become a civilian CSI, one needs to be hired by a police

A civilian crime scene investigator has no more authority in law enforcement than any other citizen on the street. Because it is not mandatory, if a civilian CSI chooses to carry a weapon, they may be required to pay for the initial shooting course and pay for a concealed weapons permit, and they must stay certified by attending regular department qualification and training. They are allowed to carry pistols like any other civilian as long as they have a permit. In addition, they are not sworn officers and do not have the arrest powers of police officers. If they had to make an arrest, they would have to do it just as any other civilian, by declaring a "citizen's arrest."

Civilian forensic specialist minimum requirements in a midsize California police department are:

Education: Equivalent to an associate of arts degree from an accredited college with major coursework in criminology, criminalistics, or a closely related field, and/or specific forensic training, and two years of full-time experience in law enforcement identification work to include crime scene investigation and/or the examination of latent print evidence.

A bachelor's degree, completion of FBI or Department of Justice (DOJ) basic and advanced fingerprint courses and/or basic and advanced field evidence technician courses, and certification as a latent print examiner and crime scene analyst are highly desired. This means an individual with these qualifications will probably get the position over a candidate with an associate of arts degree. A copy of an associate of arts degree or bachelor's degree must be submitted with a completed application.

agency. The agencies usually require a college degree in a forensic discipline and knowledge of processing crime scenes, but not all agencies have those requirements. Contact a local police department, sheriff's department, or the state police to find out if they hire civilian crime scene investigators and what their requirements are for the position.

## ONE EXAMPLE OF THE SELECTION PROCEDURE FOR A CSI

**Part I:** Candidates will be invited to an oral interview to evaluate education, training, experience, and job-related qualifications for the position. The minimum qualifying score is 70 to 80 percent. Candidates will also participate in a nonscored latent print examination practical evaluation.

**Part II:** Candidates who successfully pass Part I of the examination process will be placed on an eligibility list. The top candidate will proceed to a screening process, which will consist of a criminal records check, Department of Motor Vehicles (DMV) driving record review, personal history statement, polygraph examination, background investigation, and medical examination.

## BOSTON POLICE IDENTIFICATION TECHNICIAN

Identification technicians staff the Boston police crime scene unit. They work three shifts to provide around-the-clock crime scene response. A senior identification technician supervises them. In addition to field calls, the identification technicians provide expert services in the following areas:

· Latent fingerprint processing and examination, including entering fingerprints into the Automated Fingerprint Identification System.

· The restoration of obliterated serial numbers on firearms and other serial number–bearing devices, such as stereos, televisions, and appliances.

· Photography and physical evidence collection at postmortem examinations.

· Examination and identification of shoe and tire tracks collected from crime scenes.

· Processing, packaging, and preserving fragile or easily destroyed evidence, such as biological materials destined for examination by the DNA/serology unit.

· Separation and packaging of expended bullets and cartridge casings collected from shooting scenes, readying them for examination by the firearms/tool marks unit.

· Lifting latent fingerprints from narcotics packaging prior to analysis by the narcotics analysis unit.

Education is always required. A few agencies may require civilians to have a two-year college degree; others may require specific four-year, or graduate, degrees, such as a master of science degree in biology, chemistry, or another forensic science. Civilians are frequently employed as handwriting and fingerprint analysts.

## PROS AND CONS

Sworn crime scene investigators—that is, those who are sworn police officers—may be paid at a higher level than their civilian counterparts; they may have better fringe benefits and an available career ladder. Civilian crime scene investigators have fewer career opportunities and work in the same dangerous environment as their police officer counterparts. The civilian CSI usually must also conform to the department's background investigation standards, physical fitness requirements, and other requirements.

## GENERAL DUTIES

The crime scene investigator's duties generally depend on the individual's education, agency, and experience, and the duties vary throughout the country. In general, at major crime scenes, the crime scene investigator works with a criminal investigator in charge of the case. The

### LAS VEGAS METROPOLITAN POLICE DEPARTMENT TRAINING CLASSES

**Crime Analyst I:** This is the entry-level class and is distinguished from the crime analyst II by the performance of the more routine tasks and duties assigned to positions within the series, including responding to basic crime trend inquiries and evaluating and identifying crime series, patterns, and trends. Since this class is typically used as a training class, employees may have only limited or no directly related work experience.

The class teaches knowledge of: Research and analytical techniques used in the extraction and presentation of crime data and the development and dissemination of crime and intelligence data; investigative theory, practices, and techniques; principles of statistical analysis and mathematics; methods and principles of crime analysis; methods of research, program analysis, and report preparation; computer applications, including databases, spreadsheets, and word processing; and operational characteristics of the geographic information system (GIS). This training requires education equivalent to a bachelor's degree from an accredited college or university in criminal justice, business management, public administration, sociology, or a related field. College-level coursework in statistics and research methods is desirable.

**Crime Analyst II:** This is the full-journey level within the crime analyst series. This class is distinguished from the crime analyst I by the performance of the full range of duties as assigned, including the most technical and analytical projects. Employees at this level receive only occasional instruction or assistance as new or unusual situations arise and are fully aware of the operating procedures and policies of the work unit. Positions in this class are flexibly staffed and are normally filled from the outside by individuals with prior experience, or from within by progression from the first level. If hired at the entry level, employees are expected to progress to the second level upon successful completion of a training period of two years.

Some jurisdictions may require the equivalent to an associate of arts degree from an accredited community college with major coursework in criminal justice, forensic science, physical science, or a related field, including specialized training in crime scene investigation, and possession of, or ability to obtain, a forensic science certificate from the American Institute of Applied Science within one year from date of hire as a crime scene investigator.

### LATENT PRINT EXAMINER JOB DESCRIPTION

Montgomery County (Maryland) Department of Police position of latent print examiner. The qualifications include "completion of high school; formal training in the classification, searching, and filing of inked fingerprints and comparison; three years of experience preparing, lifting, comparing, identifying, and preserving latent prints and related evidence; and three years of experience taking, comparing, and identifying fingerprints.

"Responsibilities include comparing and identifying whole and fragmentary latent prints lifted from or developed on various and possibly unstable surfaces; testifying in court as an expert witness; using the Henry System of fingerprint classification; and classifying, searching, and identifying fingerprints accurately."

### FIREARMS/TOOL MARK EXAMINER JOB DESCRIPTION

The Las Vegas Metropolitan Police Department position of Firearms/Toolmark Examiner. "Qualifications include a bachelor's degree in criminalistics, forensic science, chemistry, biology, or related field, and three years of responsible research and practical experience working in a forensic laboratory as a professional firearms/tool mark examiner.

"Responsibilities include performing scientific and laboratory analyses on firearms and tool mark evidence, interpreting test results and forming conclusions, preparing reports, and testifying in court as an expert witness."

CSI is responsible for the thorough documentation of the scene and the identification, processing, and collection of physical evidence. The CSI needs an expertise in photography and processing of latent and patent evidence, which includes but is not limited to fingerprints, footwear, tool and tire impressions, hair and fibers, and (trace evidence) biological fluids, including collecting samples of potential DNA for analysis and blood spatter pattern analysis. Other specialties may be required. The crime scene investigator must follow the protocol for performing a systematic search of the crime scene and maintain chain of custody for the evidence collected at the scene.

## CRIME SCENE INVESTIGATOR APPLICATION

The crime scene investigator application process varies widely between agencies. The Morris County, New Jersey, Sheriff's Criminal Investigation Section's (CIS) process is a typical example of a professional law enforcement agency that employs (sworn) full-time crime scene investigators.

When a vacancy opens up in the Criminal Investigation Section due to a retirement or other reason, it is posted within the department. Sworn personnel may submit a letter of interest. They will receive a study packet of material on which they will later be tested. The test consists of three parts: a crime scene investigation test, a fingerprint test, and a fingerprint comparison test. These tests are competitive, and only the individuals with the highest scores will go before an interview committee composed of a lieutenant, a CIS sergeant, two CIS detectives, and a representative of the Police Benevolent Association. (The list of other candidates will remain active for one year, after which it is canceled.) Applicants for future openings must retest. The committee will also review the individual's in-service timecard, holiday, personal, overtime, and sick time.

The fingerprint and crime scene investigator's tests are each given a maximum of 20 percent value; the interview carries a maximum 50 percent value, and the timecard receives a 5 percent value. The applicant will receive a questionnaire, which will ask for the applicant's career goals and reasons and motivations for wanting to become a member of the Criminal Investigations Section. This questionnaire receives a 5 percent value. Once the individual is approved, he or she is enrolled in the in-house crime scene investigator's course, which is approximately a 375-hour course. The trainee must pass the in-house course with a score of at least 90 percent.

While this process varies throughout the United States, there are commonalities within the processes. The most successful way to become a crime scene investigator is to have the law enforcement and educational background first. After three or more years on the job as a law enforcement officer, the next step is to apply for a crime scene investigator position within that agency. Some CSI personnel are sworn officers who do crime scene investigation as a collateral job. In some agencies, promotion to detective is the gateway to becoming a full-time crime scene investigator.

**CRIME SCENE INVESTIGATOR TRAINING**
Crime scene investigator training, both in-service and academic, is usually offered by the law enforcement agency that employs the individual, and the agency will generally pay for specific aspects of job training. Some agencies call on the Federal Bureau of Investigation (FBI) through the FBI Academy in Quantico, Virginia, for crime scene training. The FBI will accommodate these requests at a local field office equipped to handle such requests. The training generally consists of one week of intensive forensic-geared academics taught by supervisory special agents.

In the scientific community, the crime scene investigator (referred to as a criminalist in some jurisdictions), or evidence response technician, is accepted as a forensic specialist. The educational requirements vary and are usually at least an associate degree in either criminal justice or in a forensic science, such as chemistry, biology, microbiology, math, physics, and other scientific areas. Specialists may be required to have advanced degrees and often several years of experience in the specific discipline.

Some, but not all, of the specialized techniques crime scene investigators train for include crime reconstruction, blood spatter pattern analysis, gunshot and ballistics analysis, postblast bombing evidence recovery, latent fingerprint detection and collection, hair and fiber evidence detection and collection, tool mark identification, and crime scene and evidence photography.

Although the actual training varies, in general, an experienced crime scene investigator has successfully completed several hundred hours of training in crime scene processing, which includes approximately eighty hours training in patent and latent fingerprint processing, forty hours in major death investigations, forty hours in advanced homicide investigations, forty hours in photography, forty hours in blood spatter interpretation, eighty hours of questioned document analysis, and other training courses in arson investigation and forensic pathology. In addition, some agencies may require the crime scene investigator to be certified by the Crime Scene Certification Board of the International Association for Identification within eighteen months of completing the training as a crime scene investigator.

> Evidence is anything that has been used, left, removed, altered, or contaminated during the commission of a crime.

**MORRIS COUNTY SHERIFF'S OFFICE CRIME SCENE TRAINING**
"We have a training officer with the individual at all times, and we have a specific format and training guide for all parts of our crime scene training," said one senior officer. "For example, we have a checklist for collecting evidence from a vehicle. The first things the investigator will do are approach the vehicle and conduct a visual search to ensure that no people, dangerous substances, or explosives are in the vehicle. After donning gloves and photographing the vehicle, they perform the search inside the vehicle—glove box, under seats, and so forth. We also have a standard list of evidence items not limited to loose items, papers, cans, plastics, clothing, vegetation, and receipts. We also tell them to look under floor mats; take control samples of carpets and seats; label, package, and remove all contraband; and test for blood and other bodily fluid stains.

Through the use of modern electronic technology, such as the global positioning system, a crime scene investigator can determine a precise location of evidence.

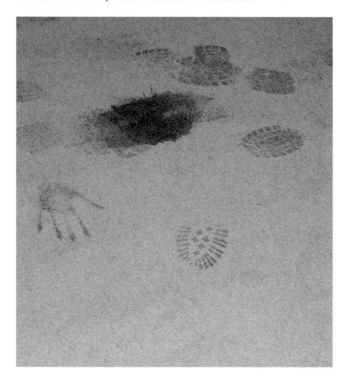

This is a training aid to illustrate suspect stains and light bloody handprints and footprints. It will be subjected to various tests to illustrate the various methods in which evidence may be obtained. These prints may be enhanced with leuco crystal violet (LCV). LCV is a coloring reagent for blood that is based on the blood-catalyzed reaction of hydrogen peroxide with LCV, whereby the colorless LCV is oxidized to the purple crystal violet.

Two FBI special agents use metal detectors to look for metal objects that may be part of a simulated crime scene, such as spent bullet casings, or metallic weapons.

What is collected at a crime scene is physical evidence, such as guns, glass, fingerprints, etc. Within this general category are the subcategories of trace evidence and impression evidence. Trace evidence is microscopic or pseudomicroscopic evidence, such as hair and paint chips. Impression evidence is evidence that is not collected, but impressions are made of it, such as a footprint or tool mark.

"We process all areas inside, such as windows, doors, handles, mirrors, steering wheel, seatbelt buckles, console, and gas tank door, and we check any compact disks and buttons for latent prints using laser or alternate light sources, Super Glue fuming, or powders as appropriate.

"On stains, we do a presumptive test for blood using luminol or phenolphthalein, even if blood is not visibly present. The obvious places we look, but not limited to these areas, are all stains, steering wheel, foot pedals, and handles and buttons. We remove and test under floorboards and between the seats and doors. They would also do a random test of the inside of the trunk," he said.

DNA is a major tool in crime scene investigation, so the investigator will swab such areas as door handles, seatbelts, and buckles. "We collect cigarette butts in a paper envelope, because as a general rule, biological evidence is best stored in paper to avoid degradation that may occur if the sample is or becomes wet. Drink containers may also yield DNA, especially the edges where lip gloss may be present," he said.

The new CSI is taught to look under the vehicle, in the wheelwells, and in the tire treads, which may reveal chunks of soil that, when analyzed, may reveal where the vehicle has been. Climate is also a factor for preserving evidence on or in a vehicle. In cold climates, if possible, the vehicle should be brought indoors and allowed to dry or warm before fingerprinting. In very warm climates, placing the vehicle indoors will help preserve heat-sensitive biological evidence such as DNA or entomological evidence.

If there is physical damage to the vehicle, it may have been involved in a hit-and-run. Paint transfer to or from an object may also occur. The CSI is taught to take paint samples from the damaged areas (for possible paint transfers from another vehicle) and exemplars from areas of the vehicle thought not to contain evidence. They must collect and store the suspect evidence separately from victim evidence.

A Morris County Sheriff's Office training officer (TO) records and has a checklist of every item covered

The Morris County Sheriff's Office is responsible for thirty-nine municipalities with a total county population of over 488,100. The criminal investigation section (CIS) and its eleven officers processed 150 autopsies and five thousand pieces of evidence, photographed and investigated 1,893 cases, collected and developed 2,700 latent fingerprints, and processed 318 vehicles. The photographic section produces approximately thirty-five hundred to four thousand photo prints a month and approximately fifty thousand a year. In one double murder, they developed 110 rolls of film, which produced 3,960 frames.

A general rule is to collect evidence in paper products (porous containers that breathe). Rarely is evidence collected in plastic, except for liquids.

with the new investigator, from the standard operating procedure (SOP) reference number, and the date of instruction, to the sign-off by the supervising training officer (STO).

"The new investigator will have to demonstrate his or her proficiency to the TO at least twice before that area is signed off by the STO," said one instructor. "When all the training is completed, the trainee signs and acknowledges that he or she has received the training and demonstrated proficiency in all the tasks initialed by the STO." All training officers who have participated in the individual's training will also sign off, acknowledging that they provided the training and witnessed the trainee demonstrate proficiency in those areas they signed off. The final sign-off is by the division commander.

Another method to determine the location of specific evidence is to use a surveyor's laser-ranging device. *FBI*

Upon successful completion of the training, the individual is placed on probation for one year. The trainee will continue to receive hands-on, in-house training and external training as appropriate. During that period, a training officer will ride along with the individual on calls for several weeks, and during this period and until the probationary period is over, the individual's crime scene reports are reviewed and critiqued. Upon successful completion of the probationary period, the individual is recommended for the rank of detective and given a salary stipend, which is rolled into their hourly rate.

## CRIME SCENE APPROACH

"No matter what type of scene," said one instructor, "we tell our detectives to secure an area as large as possible. If it is an open space, go as far back as you feel you need to. We use this approach because initially we may not know how far the scene may extend, and we need to ensure that any evidence beyond the immediate area is not compromised. It is easier to reduce the scene size later than expand it and have compromised evidence."

Determining the offender's point of entry (POE) and exit is important. "The POE is usually an important location for evidence," said one instructor. "Suspects exert a lot of energy at the POE and leave evidence—kicking, prying, crawling, glass, fibers, and so forth," said one senior investigator. "We set up one point of entry and exit for our investigators, and anyone else legally at the scene, and it should always be the least disturbed area if that is possible," he continued. "Anyone trampling around the scene may take evidence away on their shoes."

The scuff marks on the side of the door may indicate an entry point or possible struggle. A spent cartridge case was found just a few feet from the door, corroborating a witness report of shots fired.

## LOCARD'S EXCHANGE

One of the most important maxims in crime scene investigation is Locard's Exchange. Forensic scientist Edmond Locard established a principle that still guides criminal investigations today. Criminals leave traces of themselves at a crime scene and on the victim, and they take away evidence that they were present.

Obtaining evidence control samples is important. When "unknown" evidence samples, or specimens, are collected at the scene, they are believed to belong to, or have been transferred by, the suspect, and a "known,"

### FORENSIC EVIDENCE, THE SILENT WITNESS

In 1910, a Frenchman named Edmond Locard expressed this scientific principle that now bears his name—Locard's Exchange: "Whenever two objects come in contact with each other, there is always an exchange of material." This statement creates the basis for searching for trace evidence at crime scenes. However careful a criminal may be to avoid being seen or heard, he will inevitably defeat his purpose. Whenever he steps, whatever he touches, whatever he leaves, even unconsciously, will serve as silent evidence against him. Not only his fingerprints and his shoe prints, but also his hair, the fibers from his clothes, the glass he breaks, the tool marks he leaves, the paint he scratches, the blood or semen that he deposits or collects—all these and more bear mute witness against him. This evidence does not forget. It is not confused by the excitement of the moment. It is not absent because human witnesses are. It is factual evidence. Physical evidence cannot be wrong. It cannot perjure itself, and it cannot be wholly absent. Only the human failure to find, study, and understand it can diminish its value.

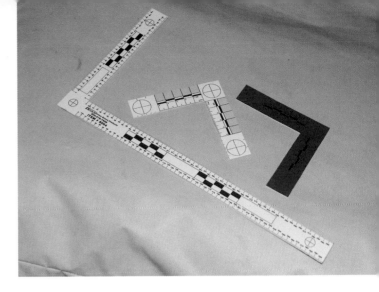

One method of identifying the location of evidence is to establish a grid at the crime scene. In this simulated crime scene, a tape measure is secured across the floor. The evidence is measured precisely from a fixed reference point, such as the west wall of the building.

These are some of the measuring rules the crime scene investigator will use. To the left is a reversible footwear and tire track scale; in the center is a photomacrographic photo-gray scale, and to the right is a photomacrographic fluorescent scale. They are positioned alongside small pieces of evidence to provide scale and for one-to-one photographs.

or exemplar, sample must be collected. This enables the forensic lab to determine if the unknown specimen is different from the known specimen, thus excluding a suspect. Hair or blood samples are collected from the victim and other persons lawfully present at the scene or at

a hospital. "Elimination prints must also be collected at the scene," said one instructor, "to rule out individuals lawfully present." With paint, known samples are collected from known surfaces. With soil, known samples are taken around the area in question.

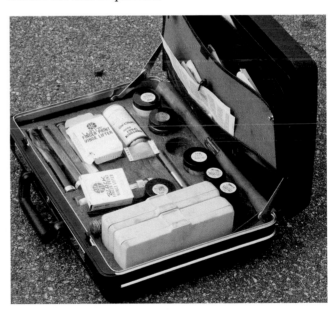

Crime scene investigators are taught that a blank piece of paper on a notepad may reveal impressions from the previous page. When writing is produced on a sheet of paper that is resting on other sheets of paper, impressions of the writing may be indented into the surface of the sheets underneath. If these indentations are deep (caused, for example, by heavy pen pressure), they may be visible to the naked eye, sometimes with the assistance of a light source shone at an oblique angle to the paper surface. There are also commercial kits available to make the indented writing visible. *Henry M. Holden*

The basic fingerprint kit comes with several colors of powder, brushes, lift tapes, ninhydrin, and should also include gloves, a mask, eye protection, and a flashlight (for dark houses and cars at night). "You can buy a complete kit for about $160," said one investigator. "However, you can get an attaché case, cut some foam cutouts, and buy all the powders and brushes for about $60."

Any objects that seem out of place should be considered potential evidence. These pliers are seemingly out of place on the floor and were marked and photographed. They were later tied in to tool marks on a window frame.

## CRIME SCENE PHOTOGRAPHY

It is axiomatic that a crime scene investigator should photograph everything. Nothing is more important in a crime scene than photography. "You can never take too many photographs," said one instructor. "And don't forget the ceiling. If the assailant beat the victim with a baseball bat, removed the body, and cleaned up the blood on the floor, it is likely he forgot to clean the cast-off blood from the ceiling."

"Nighttime photography can be challenging," said an investigator. "We sometimes call on the fire department to light the scene. When we don't have the fire department, we will use whatever light is available. If we have a tripod with us, we can always set the camera on it and take a timed shot using the bulb feature on the camera."

In agencies where 35mm film is used, the first frame on each roll of film should be the identification of the crime location, date, the investigator's name, and agency. Some agencies use preprinted cards that can be filled in with a magic marker pen and photographed.

"It is important that you get your name on the first frame of every roll," said the instructor. "This will allow the photo developers to associate all the rolls to a specific investigator at the scene. If you don't have this card, use your business card.

"The next thing to remember is not to mix cases on the same roll. Film is relatively cheap. You do not want a

Videotaping crime scenes is becoming commonplace. The FBI special agent evidence response technician is videotaping one of the rooms in a simulated crime scene, where a booby trap was found hanging over the doorway.

defense attorney getting a subpoena for the roll of film on a homicide case and seeing a convenience store robbery on the first eight frames." Photographs are not what a case is built on, but they do supplement the case report. The photo freezes, or memorializes, the scene at a point in time, and the scene will never look as it did at the time of the crime.

"The very next frame should be a wide shot showing the yellow tape, or other scene barriers, indicating that the crime scene has been secured," said one instructor. "The easiest way to blow a case is to have the defense attorney cast a reasonable doubt that the crime scene was not secured properly. Crime scene contamination can mislead an investigation, can be a defense attorney's best defense, and may lead to the possibility of getting the case thrown out of court," he said.

In fact, photographs are so important that some agencies will use two photographers at a major crime scene. One will back up the other person in case the film is lost or processed improperly.

"Never," said one instructor, "and I stress never, move an object or clean up any debris to get a better shot

Detective Mike Puzio instructs a new detective in crime scene vehicle photography. "Photograph the overall scene, skid or gouge marks, the four sides of the vehicle, damage to the vehicle, tire condition, speedometer, anything under the vehicle, and the vehicle identification number (VIN)," he said. "Also, make depth-of-field photos—i.e., row of cars with one in focus, depth-of-field row of cars with all in focus, overall scene with an item of evidence, and a close-up of the item of evidence are all photos needed for the case."

The first photo taken at the crime scene, after the identifying frame, should be the overall view of the scene. Two new crime scene investigators practice their photo skills in the parking lot of the Morris County Sheriff's Criminal Investigation Section.

of the object. It taints the scene and may present an untenable situation for the prosecution. If someone hands you a gun they found nearby, don't ask them to put it back. Photograph it, tag it, bag it, noting who turned it in, and where the individual said he found it."

Detective Mike Puzio explains the effects of bright sunlight on photographs. "I tell all the detectives to always carry spare batteries for their camera. Moreover, in the winter don't keep them in your patrol unit, but put them in an inner pocket, close to your body heat. Nothing will sap the battery strength faster than cold weather."

## DIGITAL MEDIA
More agencies are switching to digital photography since many courts are now agreeing that there are safeguards to maintain the original content of the unedited images. The procedure for photographing a scene is the same as for analog film; one or more Compact Flash cards per crime scene, as needed—the same as film media. Digital media is less costly than analog since about four hundred high-resolution images can be stored on a 1-gigabyte Compact Flash card, which may later be erased and reused, depending on the agency's procedures. Generally, these images will be transferred to a CD to store the original photos for the case file.

## QUESTIONED DOCUMENT ANALYSIS
One area where civilians are frequently used is in questioned document analysis, often involving handwriting comparison and analysis. The skill is generally acquired through an intensive two-week course at the Federal Law Enforcement Training Center in Glynco, Georgia, and then followed by a two-year apprenticeship and additional in-house training.

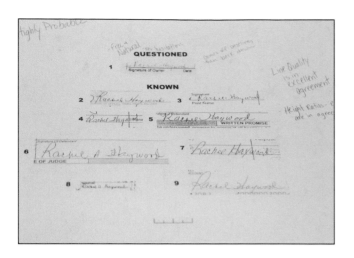

When questioned document signatures are an issue, document examiners must take into account if the individual is sick, on medication, or if there are other factors that may alter the outcome of the samples. *Morris County Sheriff's Office*

Questioned documents are first examined before ninhydrin is applied to the note or envelope because ninhydrin may reveal fingerprints but may make the detail of the writing unusable. *Morris County Sheriff's Office*

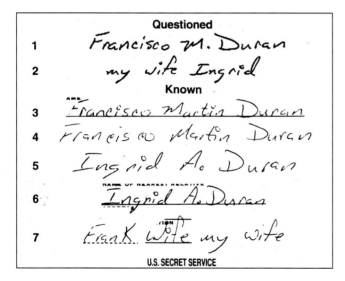

This U.S. Secret Service training aid illustrates that a suspect may be asked to write and rewrite some information many times. Eventually, if the suspect is the forger, he will get tired and unknowingly fall back to his natural writing style, which will be compared with the questioned document. *U.S. Secret Service via Morris County Sheriff's Office*

Detectives Al Dekler and Laura Valente, both trained as document examiners, are examining a questioned document.

"While DNA and fingerprints are absolute, hand-writing analysis is a tool that is not always conclusive. It is generally not enough to get a search warrant on a handwriting sample," said one instructor.

**Results from a handwriting analysis fall into five categories: no indication of a match, an indication, probable match, highly probable match, and identical.**

An administrative worksheet should be part of every major crime scene. It should list those investigators on the scene, what their responsibilities are, what evidence is collected, and more.

"I tell my students to get as many handwriting samples as possible. Get originals and, if possible, unsolicited exemplars. Originals will show pen lift and fade [as the pen leaves the paper]; photo copies will not reveal these very important clues. The best example for our purposes is generally a job application or a written report where the individual was not under any pressure," he said.

Solicited exemplars are more difficult. The suspect knows what the investigator is looking for and may try to disguise his handwriting. "One thing I stress," said one instructor, "is never show the suspect the original document. We had an insurance fraud case where the individual using the name 'Ricki' signed the original document. The suspect signed the name, spelling it 'Ricky.' We got him on one letter. Sometimes it is the smallest clue that can break a case.

"To get a match to a suspect, we may have to ask him to fill out some forms where he will write the same letters, numbers, or handwriting that is on the questioned document," continued the instructor. "The handwriting samples should try to re-create the size and environment of the original document. We are trying to match apples to apples. For example, since he knows we are trying to match his handwriting he will try to fake his usual writing style, so we may ask him to write and rewrite some information many times. Eventually, he will get

tired and unknowingly fall back to his own natural writing style," the instructor said. Forensic document specialists must also take into account if the individual is sick or on medication, or other factors that may alter the outcome of the samples.

### DUSTING AND LIFTING IMPRESSIONS

Proper dusting for print impressions is an art. The two techniques generally used for finger impressions are spinning a fingerprint brush, where it is twirled between

A fingerprint is the impression or mark left by the underside of the tips of the fingers or thumbs. The impression is formed by a pattern of ridges on the skin surface and is unique for each individual.

In addition to powders, cyanoacrylate and iodine are examples of the chemicals used to develop latent prints on nonporous surfaces, or for prints that are not fresh. Using cyanoacrylate, or iodine fuming, can cause the hidden print to develop. The resulting images can then be photographed and processed.

A detective lifts prints from a side-view mirror. Criminals will automatically touch several parts of a vehicle including the side mirror, the seat adjuster, and the rearview mirror, and it is not uncommon to find prints on these objects.

Several detectives dust a car while another prepares to photograph any developed prints, all under the watchful eyes of Detective Corporal Bill Stitt, the instructor.

Detectives dust the glass on a suspect vehicle. Glass is easy to develop prints on but sometimes provides little contrast. With black powder, a blank white sheet of paper placed on the other side of the glass will provide the contrast necessary to photograph the print.

Ninhydrin is a chemical substance that reveals latent fingerprints on porous surfaces, such as paper, cardboard, and raw wood, by reacting with amino acids in the fingerprints. It reacts in ten to twenty minutes, developing a purplish image that may be photographed. Ninhydrin will eventually fade, making the image unusable so it must be photographed immediately after its development. Ninhydrin should be used in an open, well-ventilated area or in a sealed and vented laboratory environment. Ninhydrin may be applied up to three times to enhance the image.

Iodine fuming is a method, albeit falling out of use, of developing latent prints on paper, cardboard, and many other paper-type surfaces. The iodine develops the print from the fats left behind from the skin. The print will develop with a yellow-brown color, and because iodine fuming reacts to different components of residue, it will not interfere with subsequent applications of ninhydrin. Another compound falling from use is silver nitrate. In the opinion of crime scene investigators, silver nitrate and iodine fuming results are no better than from the use of ninhydrin.

A lab technician applies a ninhydrin spray to a threat note. Ninhydrin is an amino acid reagent that may be applied to porous surfaces in a variety of solutions to develop latent prints. Ninhydrin has been recognized since the turn of the twentieth century as a reagent for detecting amino acids. However, it was not until the mid-1950s that ninhydrin was used to develop latent prints. When ninhydrin comes into contact with amino acids in fingerprint residue, the reaction yields a purple image. Nitrile gloves, a lab coat, safety goggles, and breathing mask should be worn when working with ninhydrin indoors. *FBI*

two fingers, or sweeping the brush. "If the investigator is too vigorous in applying the powder, he or she can damage the print and render it unusable," said the instructor. "Too much powder can also present problems, such as blocking out some of the fine details needed to make the impression clear. I tell my students either method is useful, and to use whichever method he or she gets better results, but always dust with the lines of the print, not against them."

While there are various colors of dusting powders and lifters (special adhesive tape that lifts the developed impression) available, black or white powders and lifters will provide all the contrasts needed. Fluorescent powders, while they will glow under certain lights, also create fuzzy areas, especially around the edges, and make them harder to read.

"I tell my students that if you can lift a print from a light bulb, you can probably lift a print from anything. Then I have them practice until they can lift a print from

a light bulb," said the instructor. "The offender will often unscrew a light bulb until it goes out without actually removing it, and leave a print behind." The need for this skill was demonstrated to this writer when a crime scene investigator had to dust and remove prints from a round doorknob at a burglary and theft scene.

## AUTOMATED FINGERPRINT IDENTIFICATION SYSTEM

The Automated Fingerprint Identification System (AFIS) and the federal (Integrated) IAFIS are computer search programs for a match of a fingerprint(s) submitted to those of convicted offenders on file. The computer runs an algorithm that compares individual points on a print. It looks at size and distance between ridgelines. The computer will usually produce twenty-five prints with similar characteristics. It is then the job of a fingerprint examiner using a magnifying glass to do a comparison, looking for an exact match. Fingerprints are so unique

*Continued on page 54*

Detective Mike Puzio discusses the outcome of a fingerprint lift with two students. "Identifying fingerprints basically starts with pattern recognition," he said.

Magnetic powder is also used to lift prints from a surface. When used properly, it will leave a clean, well-defined print. Magnetic powder is black volcanic ash print powder mixed with magnetized iron filings. It can be used successfully on any porous surface, such as paper, cardboard, and wood.

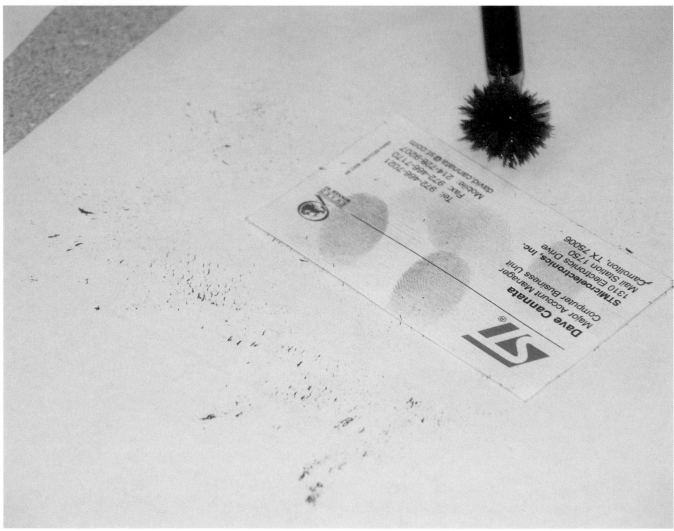

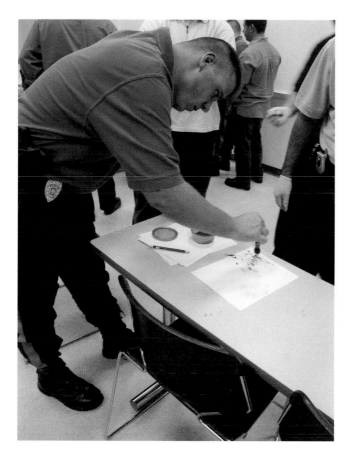

This detective practices magnetic powder dusting. The applicator is not a brush but a small rod roughly the size of a pencil that has a magnet on one end. When extended, the rod picks up the magnetized filings, which are then dusted on the impression. Retracting the rod causes the filings to drop off.

This detective applies a black print powder to the side window of a vehicle. "I tell my students," said one instructor, "think about how you would break into a vehicle. What would you touch, the side mirror, radio, would you adjust the seat? Then start developing those areas."

This impression, revealed by dusting at a burglary crime scene, was later identified as a fabric impression, most likely from someone who closed the drawer with one knee.

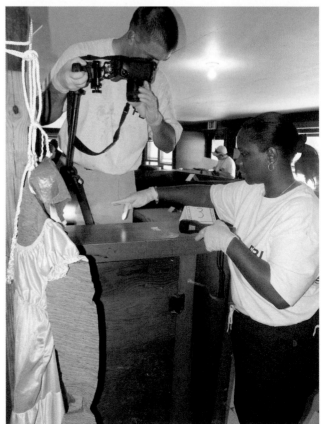

While one FBI evidence response technician adjusts the camera for a photograph, the other uses a technique called oblique lighting on the shelf to reveal a light footwear impression. ERT members are selected within each FBI field office through a competitive career board process. Candidates are selected largely based upon FBI and prior employment experiences in a forensic area. ERT is an ancillary position except for twenty full-time senior team leaders in major field offices.

Fingerprint powders come in several colors, but black and white are the most commonly used. "Whenever dusting, I tell investigators to wear a mask," said one instructor. "The white powder is called 'indestructible white'; the black powder is made from volcanic ash, and ninhydrin, which is also used to develop prints, comes in liquid and spray form, and is poisonous. Ninhydrin should be used either outside or in a well-ventilated lab."

This door was jimmied using first a screwdriver (near the door latch), and then a larger pry bar below. Tool marks, which appear on vertical surfaces such as door frames, cannot be cast by pouring compounds into them. Casting materials, such as Mikrosil, may be used since the epoxy comes in two different compounds and is mixed together into a pastelike consistency and applied to the marks.

*Continued from page 49*

Detective Ed Crooker of the Morris County Sheriff's Criminal Investigation Section is accessing the New Jersey State Police Automated Fingerprint Identification System (AFIS). AFIS has over three million prints. It is still up to the fingerprint examiner to review each one and determine if there is a match. "It would take my whole career to match one print against the old card files in this database," said Crooker. "AFIS can do it usually in less than a half-hour." Prints are kept in the AFIS database until the statute of limitations on the crime expires, except for homicide, where there is no statute of limitations.

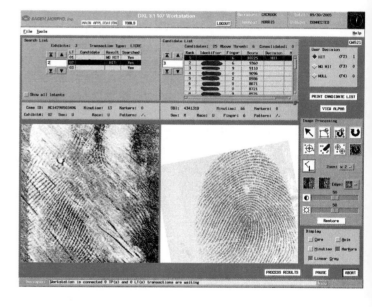

that as few as four matching points on a print have been accepted in court as proof that the individual on trial left the impressions at the scene.

"How the officer rolls the print," said one instructor, "is important. If there is too much ink or too little it will affect the computer's ability to read and interpret the data, and our ability to find a match."

### SIMULATED TRAINING

As part of a crime scene investigator's final exam, in a simulated situation, the trainee must exhibit the ability to conduct a portion of a preliminary crime scene investigation that would minimally include:

    A. Ensuring the trainee's safety and the safety of others present

    B. Identifying the extent of the crime scene

    C. Ensuring medical aid for the injured

The Automated Fingerprint Identification System (AFIS) will return the suspect print along with up to twenty-five other possible candidates in its database. Positioned alongside each other for immediate comparison, the screen is printed out to make a magnified comparison. *Morris County Sheriff's Office*

Luminol is a chemical that is capable of detecting blood stains diluted up to ten thousand times. It is used to identify blood that has been removed from a given area. It is a common and valuable tool for crime scene investigators at an altered crime scene.

D. Containing area; preserving crime scene

E. Identifying and preserving evidence

Locating and identifying suspects, witnesses, and victims

G. Conducting initial interviews

H. Completing field notes, indicating conditions and events

## WORKING CONDITIONS

The crime scene investigator should respond to calls for crime scene services as quickly as good judgment and safety allows. He or she may be required to process scenes of major crimes at any hour of the day or night, and under all weather conditions. Approximately 70 percent of crime scene investigators' time is spent photographing and processing crime scenes, packaging and transporting evidence, and attending autopsies, and he or she may assist the pathologist with the collection of physical evidence from the body, as well as take the victim's fingerprints. He or she may attend briefings and conferences with the police agencies requesting assistance. The remaining time is spent preparing investigative reports, testifying in court, receiving continuing education, instructing classes, and maintaining equipment in a state of readiness.

Crime scene searches are often performed by extensive kneeling, stooping, reaching, and climbing. Heavy lifting may be required at times. He or she will handle objects of varying weight and shape and must, therefore, be agile and in good physical condition. The CSI must also maintain his or her equipment and keep up to date on all forensic techniques and methodologies in their specialty. For crime scene investigators, collecting evidence from crime scenes can sometimes be distressing and unpleasant. Crime scene investigators in general often work crime scenes where there is evidence of violent behavior with blood, body parts, and the mutilation of human bodies. Even though crime scene investigators may

The following are some of the specialized techniques a crime scene investigator employs:
- Crime scene reconstruction
- Blood spatter pattern analysis
- Gunshot reconstruction and ballistics evidence
- Detection and recovery of human remains and buried remains recovery
- Postblast/bombing crime scene evidence recovery
- Latent fingerprint detection and collection
- Cyanoacrylate fuming for latent prints
- Trace evidence vacuum processing
- Hair and fiber evidence detection and collection
- Electrostatic dust-print lifting
- DNA evidence recovery
- Ground metal detection and ground-penetrating radar
- Casting of shoe and tire impressions and tool mark evidence
- Evidence collection and packaging
- Crime scene and evidence photography
- Crime scene diagramming and sketching

A crime scene investigator must be alert to three dangerous situations: a terrorist attack, weapons of mass destruction, and a methamphetamine lab, which has the potential for explosive and hazardous material scattered around the scene.

## SEARCH AND SEIZURE OF EVIDENCE

The Fourth Amendment protects people against unreasonable searches and seizures. A CSI may need a search warrant to gather evidence away from the crime scene and may need a warrant to confront a suspect not present at the crime scene. If the evidence recovered at a crime scene implicates an individual, the warrant must state the probable cause for the search, that the items covered in the warrant are part of the crime, and where they may be found. There are exceptions to this. For example, it is legal to search for evidence in abandoned property, such as garbage pails, or materials such as coffee cups left in a public place and in plain sight.

This FBI hazardous material response team (HMRT) responded to a simulated biological crime scene and must decontaminate it before removing their protective clothing. The individual will scrub with soap and water and then wash down in the second area of the tank separated by the yellow wall.

develop a tolerance for horribly mutilated bodies and the coppery stench of blood, some agencies will rotate the crime scene investigator to other areas of police work, as the constant exposure to the traumas extracts a psychological toll on the investigator.

After formal training, the new CSI will spend years learning the nuances of crime scene investigating. Additional training is an ongoing necessity as technology continues to develop. The actual crime scene is where much of this knowledge is acquired.

**CSI BURGLARY CHECKLIST**

1. Photograph
2. Tool marks
3. Paint standards
4. Safe insulation standards
5. Footprints
6. Tire tracks
7. Fingerprints (latents)
8. Glass standards
9. Soil standards
10. Hairs and fibers
11. Other evidence relative to crime

## HOMICIDE CHECKLIST

1. 1–9 on burglary checklist
2. Hair standard
3. Fingernail scrapings
4. Blood standards
5. Blood sample (scene)
6. Close-up photos of wounds
7. Clothing of victim
8. Clothing of suspect
9. Other evidence relative to crime
10. Weapons
11. Major case prints
12. Identification photos
13. Attend autopsy/collect evidence

A senior detective in the Morris County Sheriff's Office CIS has more than 2,200 hours of forensic training after his college degree and basic police training. Others in his unit have over 800 hours of forensic training in addition to their basic police course and college degrees.

Detective Bruce Dunn collects the bagged evidence while Detective James Rae documents the collection on digital media.

# THREE

Detective Laura Valente of the Morris County Sheriff's Criminal Investigation Section takes a close-up photograph of the suspected origin of the fire. It is clear that the fire was extremely hot, and the area Valente is photographing has nothing but globs of melted metal. Often, the reason for arson is to get rid of evidence and cover up another crime.

# The Crime Scene

The crime scene had blood everywhere, and investigators could not tell if it all came from the victim. Once the escape route of the killer was discovered, it was clear that the killer had been hurt. This is fragile evidence that must be photographed and collected immediately. Rain or an increase in temperature will melt the snow and the evidence. Prior to casting with dental stone or other casting material, SnowPrint Wax may be sprayed into the impression.

The scene of the crime may be a room, the five-mile trail of a disintegrating airliner, or the hard drive of a computer. It may be international in scope and include dozens of physical locations and individuals, thousands of exhibits, and nearly as many witness statements. However, the actual crime scene may have little resemblance to the physical layout visible at the scene, and often, the size of the scene has little relation to the time required to process it.

All crime scenes have two areas, or perimeters—the primary area, where the crime was committed, or where the victim is located, and a secondary area, which may encompass other rooms of the building, the planning area, vehicle(s), and access or escape routes. Initially, the secondary area may not always be completely or properly identified, or protected. There may also be an extended perimeter, where the suspect may have discarded evidence while fleeing the scene.

Establishing and protecting the boundaries of a crime scene may be a challenging task. For major crimes, CSI personnel will set up a command post beyond the secondary area, where certain personnel may observe the process but not commingle with investigators or potential evidence. If the scene involves hostages, bombs, a plane crash, or weapons of mass

For crimes scenes, such as the World Trade Center or an airline crash, investigators use checklist formats in response to the event. The World Trade Center attacks created a horrific crime scene with over twenty-eight hundred dead and missing victims. The FBI assigned over seven thousand special agents and over 250 laboratory and other personnel to the case. They made over fifty thousand photographs of the wreckage of the twin towers and sifted through tons of debris. Many law enforcement agencies, such as the Morris County Sheriff's Office Criminal Investigation Section, sent their personnel to the site to assist with search warrants, crime scene processing, etc. *James Tourtellotte, Immigration Customs and Enforcement*

Morris County's Sheriff's Office seal

A crime scene in a suburban area is taped off to protect any evidence that the crime scene investigators may find valuable. At this crime scene, the outer perimeter of the scene is the house itself, and only authorized personnel are permitted inside the tape.

destruction (WMD), the perimeters will be defined by a SWAT team, bomb squad, hazmat unit, the FBI, or the National Transportation Safety Board (NTSB).

## SECURING THE CRIME SCENE

The first responder must assume that the scene is unsecured and dangerous until proven otherwise. He or she must weigh all the issues and make immediate decisions based on the situation. For example, if

Evidence found at crime scenes fall into seven major groups: weapons, blood, imprints or impressions, tool marks, dust and dirt traces, questioned documents, and miscellaneous trace or transfer evidence.

This foot impression in snow is fragile and subject to degrading if the temperature rises above freezing. A CSI applies a chemical to stabilize the print prior to its casting.

weather or environmental conditions pose a danger to the evidence, the evidence must be protected and secured as soon as possible.

The first responder must also secure and protect the scene from any unwanted intrusion. Such intrusions can disturb, contaminate, or destroy evidentiary material before a proper search is made.

For faster access to law enforcement databases, such as the National Crime Information Center (NCIC), law enforcement is turning to wireless technology. Portable computers at crime scenes are now integrated with high-speed wireless wide-area network (WWAN) technology with connection options that allow the user to switch between 802.11b/g, Bluetooth, and WWAN, depending on whether the user wishes to connect to a hot spot, peripheral, or nationwide network. This high-speed access is protected by Encrypt TAC, a secure wireless communications solution that exceeds the FBI's Criminal Justice Information System (CJIS) requirements without compromising security.

Safety is of paramount importance at any crime scene. The CSI must wear appropriate protective clothing and booties to prevent crime scene contamination and must remain alert for any hazard that can be inhaled or break unprotected skin areas.

## CSI TEAM LEADER

Every crime scene is unique, and processing a scene is often a complex undertaking, combining multiple forensic specialties. For a large crime scene, a team leader usually assumes control and ensures safety of personnel and security at the scene. He or she will ensure personnel use appropriate protective equipment and follow standard procedures to protect them from health hazards, which may be present in the form of blood-borne pathogens, other body fluids, gas, chemicals, or other hazardous materials.

The team leader may determine the search patterns and make appropriate assignments for team members in keeping with their training, aptitude, and experience. Personnel may be assigned two or more responsibilities. The ultimate purpose of a crime scene search is to collect evidence that links a suspect to the crime or victim. Escape routes often yield weapons and tools discarded by the offender. Other unusual places, such as crawl spaces, a basement refrigerator, or a bathroom vanity, must also be considered during the search. Investigators will pay special attention to any areas or objects that seem to have received attention by the offender and seem out of context or do not fit into the scene.

The type of terrain usually dictates the search pattern used, and the search usually begins from the primary scene outward, toward the probable access and escape routes. The team leader will make decisions on the kinds of lab tests needed and whether any additional forensic specialists may be needed, such as a blood spatter analyst.

## CRIME SCENE CONTAMINATION

One of the problems a crime scene investigator may encounter is crime scene contamination, caused by the public, the victim, curious officers, detectives, supervisors, the press, or others. Most CSI personnel responsible for processing crime scene evidence find the same problems repeated by the same personnel or officers. "One partial solution to this dilemma," said one investigator, "is to ask those who want to get a closer look to leave a set of elimination prints. With the higher brass, it is sometimes a matter of being a diplomat."

After the crime scene is secure, a basic crime scene protocol of interviewing, examining, photographing, sketching, and processing begins. These steps may vary, and many smaller agencies often cross-train their investigators in these tasks.

### Interviewing

Generally speaking, there are two types of detectives—people detectives, who canvass and interview suspects, witnesses, and the victims (if possible), and thing detectives, who are crime scene investigators who collect and process evidence. These individuals may be called crime scene investigators, emergency response technicians, crime scene technicians, investigators, or other similar titles.

The detectives must interview the first responders, the victim if possible, and witnesses. He or she will ask what allegedly happened, what crime allegedly took place, and how the crime was allegedly committed. The information may not be factual at this point, but it will give the investigators a base from which to start.

**The twelve-step crime scene approach used by some agencies:**

- · Basic premises
- · Preparation
- · Approach
- · Secure and protect
- · Preliminary survey
- · Evaluate physical evidence
- · Narrative
- · Photography
- · Sketch
- · Search, record, and physical-evidence collection
- · Final survey
- · Release

Detectives will also canvass the neighborhood in an attempt to seek witnesses who may not know they have useful information about the crime. "Motive and opportunity, not theories, are the best types of information witnesses can provide," said one investigator, "so it may be practical to canvass after one has identified some suspects or the victim, at least." Personnel who canvass should be especially alert to anyone who appears unusually nervous, since such nonverbal reactions may be interpreted as a "soft" confession. The same applies to any onlookers or witnesses questioned at the scene.

### *Developing a General Theory*

Examining the crime scene is the second step in the protocol. The investigator examines the scene to identify possible items of an evidentiary nature, the point of entry and exit, and to get the general layout of the crime scene. The CSI will attempt to read and reconstruct the events as they happened before, during, and immediately following the commission of the crime, in order to establish the type and location of evidence. After doing an initial walk-through, the investigator may form several tentative assertions of the crime and focus on a likely

sequence of events. Examining the scene will help determine if the assertions may be substantiated by what the crime scene technician observes.

### *Photographing the Crime Scene*

Photographing the crime scene is necessary to establish a permanent record of what the scene looks like and to record items of possible evidence and their location for possible use in court.

The photographer is a key member of the crime scene team. Although photographing the crime scene is the third step in the protocol, many forensic investigators consider it the most important step, and it begins when the investigator approaches the scene. "You get only one chance to photograph the crime scene," said one

Evidence is first photographed where found, then marked with an evidence marker and photographed again. Nothing should be removed from the area of the evidence, even scraps of plastic, to clean up the photograph. The golden rule of crime scene management is: Do not move anything.

Some crime scenes have been booby-trapped, and crime scene investigators must take precautions when entering the scene.

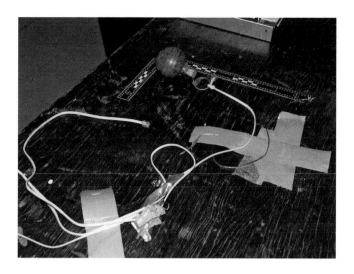

After another booby trap was safely removed, it is photographed against a scale before it is packaged and transported for laboratory analysis.

Detective Bruce Dunn of the Morris County Sheriff's Criminal Investigation Section and Detective Chris Thompson of the Hanover Township Police Department exchange notes after processing a crime scene.

The first photograph used as evidence was presented at a trial in 1859 when it was used to prove a fraudulent property title. In 1875, the first traffic accident photograph was entered as evidence. The plaintiff tried to prove he had been forced to drive his horse and buggy off the road to avoid a deep mud hole.

investigator. "You cannot take too many photographs," he said, "especially of a major crime scene."

The camera can record details of a crime scene with accuracy unmatched by a crime scene investigator's notes. It can record fragile or transient evidence such as water droplets, footprints, blood in melting snow, or bite marks. Photographs and video recordings can provide a jury with vivid pictures of the crime scene.

Crime scene photographers must have a proper understanding of lighting, distortion, and various focal planes to properly photograph the scene. The crime scene photographer may use both 35mm analog color and black-and-white (contrast) film, 200- to 400-speed film, tripods to keep close-up shots steady, and an assortment of rulers to put the objects in the photographs in perspective and scale.

There are three potential general ranges of photographs made at a crime scene: overview, midrange, and close-up. The photos that are overview (locale and

The postmortem examination of a skeleton after years of being buried is a challenge for a pathologist because of the advanced levels of decay over many parts of the body. *FBI*

Photographing human remains is important to demonstrate the original condition of the corpse. Close-up photos are essential as the body will continue to decay, and eventually what identifying characteristics remained will be lost. *FBI*

approach route) and midrange (ten to twenty feet) may help establish the "MO" or *modus operandi*, the criminal's method of operation, or how the crime was committed.

There are two general types of photographs: overlapping and progressive. Overlapping photographs are a series of photos taken in a panoramic or clockwise direction. Each photo overlaps slightly to show the overall scene. Progressive photography starts at a fixed point (i.e., entrance to the scene). The photographer makes photographs of each piece of evidence as he or she moves toward the scene, progressively getting closer in each photo.

For indoor photography, the crime scene photographer will likely use the four corners method to record the scene. The first photo is from the doorway of the room in which the victim was found. He or she will then photograph the scene from each of the four corners of the room.

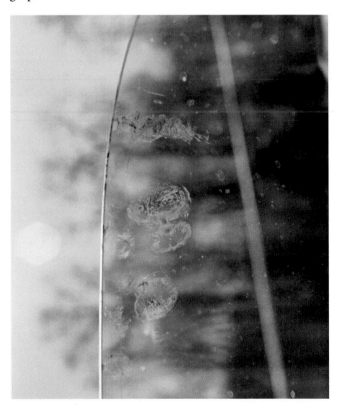

Bloody fingerprints left on glass discovered at the scene of a homicide may be a major clue and may likely be those left by the killer. The blood, however, may also be the victim's. If the prints are not in AFIS, the laboratory will submit the DNA found in the blood to the Combined DNA Index System (CODIS). *Morris County Sheriff's Office*

*Modus operandi*, or "MO," describes the behaviors, weapons, tools, and strategies a criminal uses to commit a crime. The concept of the MO was developed in 1880 in England. It described a system for identifying a criminal's MO that included location of the crime, time, method of transportation to and from the crime scene, point of entry, method of entry, tools used during the crime, objects taken from the crime scene, criminal's ability, accomplices, and unusual features of the crime. MO is learned behavior.

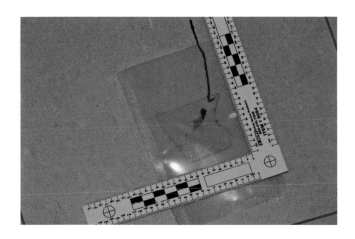

This fiber was found on a hook and photographed. It was then bagged and placed next to a scale to put its size in perspective and was photographed again.

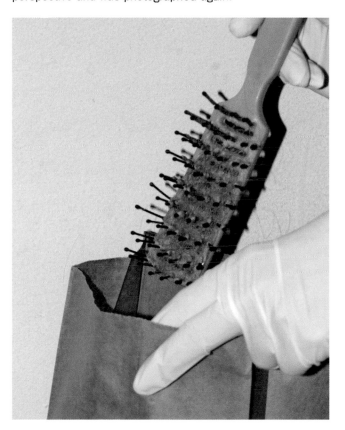

DNA may be found on almost any object handled by a person. Hairbrushes are potentially rich sources of both mtDNA and nDNA. There may also be fingerprints on the brush handle. "There are only three surfaces that a CSI cannot develop prints," said one instructor, "running water, air, and the surface you don't bother with."

"Photograph the ceiling, too," said one investigator. "If the scene appears to have been cleaned up, the killer may not have noticed that the tire iron he used probably threw blood up to the ceiling. If you come across a substance that looks like blood, photograph it first, and then do a presumptive test."

The photographer will then photograph the victim. Bodies are photographed from five angles: head to feet, right side, feet to head, left side, and straight down from above, with close-ups of the injuries.

The photographer will then concentrate on the surrounding area, which may include any potential weapons, evidence of a fight, such as spilled drinks, broken glassware, a jimmied door or window locks, and even ashtrays and their contents. "If you can see it," said one investigator, "you can photograph it."

Detective Valente has just arrived at a suspected crime scene and is taking overall photos of the area. These photos are important because they show the scene before it is processed. The photographs may also show the presence or absence of evidence. "Photography is everything," said one crime scene instructor. "You can never take too many photographs."

Detective Valente photographs the suspected arson scene from all angles. The intense heat melted the metal filing cabinets stored in the trailers, leading one to suspect that this may be arson. Detective Valente will wait for the arson investigator to arrive, and if he determines it was arson, she will take directions from the arson specialist on what evidence to photograph and how to do it.

If the investigator's assertions of the case indicate that the intruder may have forcibly entered a building through a window, then the crime scene investigator must examine the window area for footwear patterns, tool or pry marks, fingerprints, and trace evidence. Upon finding such items, the investigator will photograph their location and possibly make a sketch and notes showing the exact location of the evidence. This mixing of the steps in the protocol may continue throughout the processing of the crime scene.

High-resolution digital cameras are gaining in popularity, and with safeguards against altering original images, the courts are allowing more digital photography of

evidence. The principle of digital photography is the same as the 35mm camera. An advantage of digital photography is the immediate viewing and feedback of the image, instead of waiting hours or longer for the photographs to be developed.

The digital camera used in crime scene photography should be a single-lens reflex (through-the-lens) type with five or more megapixels of resolution, close-up capabilities, and a removable flash unit. The higher the pixel resolution, the more detail is captured. This is important when photographing small items of evidence. In addition, the difference in megapixels is important when making hard-copy prints for the case papers and

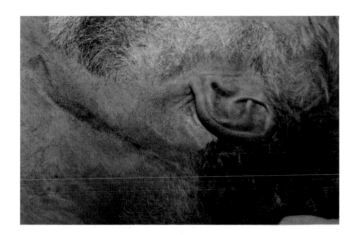

In most deaths by hanging, the individuals die from asphyxia and not a severed vertebral column and spinal cord. Marks on the skin of the neck above and below the ligature mark shows petechial hemorrhaging created when the ligature tightens and breaks the blood vessels beneath the skin. The cord will move during the victim's struggle, and the marks left will probably be larger than the ligature itself in some areas. The ligature should be removed only in the presence of, or under the direction of, the medical examiner. Close-up photos are essential for establishing the corpus delicti (the body of facts that shows physical evidence, such as a corpse) of a criminal act. *Morris County Sheriff's Office*

court presentations. Five megapixels yield a good 8x10 print, and eight megapixels or higher will yield a good 11x14 print or larger.

### *Diagramming/Sketching the Crime Scene*

Sketching the crime scene is the fourth step in the protocol and may be done concurrent with the photography or after the scene has been photographed. Diagrams or sketches provide permanent records of items, conditions, distance, and size relationships. Typically, a sketch will include at least the specific location, date, time, case number, preparer's name, and weather and lighting conditions.

A sketch illustrates the layout of the crime scene or identifies the exact position of the victim or evidence within the crime scene. A major crime scene always has sketches made and filed with the case papers. A sketch may not be completed in every case; however, some form of sketching usually occurs in most cases.

One or more of four types of sketches may be made: an overhead sketch (often called the bird's-eye view or

Crime Scene Log Sheet

Town __OXVILLE__     Crime __MURDER 2C:11-3__

Location _____

Case/IR # __12175-1__     Date __12-17-05__

| Name | Department | Time In | Time Out | Job Function |
|------|-----------|---------|----------|--------------|
| Craig Dunn | OPD | 0230 | 11:15A | CSI |
| Tina Henry | OPD | 0230 | 11:15A | CSI |
| Mary Lee | OPD | 0230 | 11:15A | CSI |
| J Peterson | OPD | 0230 | 11:15A | CSI |
| Bill Jenkins | OPD | 0245 | 11:15A | CSI |
|  |  |  |  |  |
|  |  |  |  |  |
|  |  |  |  |  |
|  |  |  |  |  |
|  |  |  |  |  |
|  |  |  |  |  |
|  |  |  |  |  |
|  |  |  |  |  |
|  |  |  |  |  |
|  |  |  |  |  |
|  |  |  |  |  |
|  |  |  |  |  |
|  |  |  |  |  |
|  |  |  |  |  |
|  |  |  |  |  |
|  |  |  |  |  |
|  |  |  |  |  |

The entry and exit log to a crime scene is as important as any evidence discovered at the crime scene. It may be necessary to present one or more individuals in court or have them donate exemplar samples to be eliminated as a suspect.

floor plan, depicting the scene as it would be seen in an aerial photograph); an exploded-view sketch (resembles the scene if all the walls were removed); an elevation sketch (looking at the scene from the side); and a perspective sketch (three-dimensional, and usually requires some drafting experience).

A latent print is an impression not readily visible made by contact of the hands or feet with a surface, resulting in the transfer of materials from the skin to that surface.

Sketches contain physical measurements of the entire scene, and if there is a body, evidence measurements may be taken from two fixed points. Sketches may also contain a legend that matches each piece of evidence

Transient evidence is evidence which, by its very nature or the conditions at the scene, will lose its evidentiary value if not preserved and protected (e.g., blood in the snow).

Two FBI evidence response technicians set up a camera for a difficult photo of a partial handprint. An ERT typically consists of a team leader and about seven members, all of whom have designated responsibilities, including those of team leader, photographer, sketch preparer, evidence log recorder, evidence collector/processor, and often specialists such as bomb technicians or forensic anthropologists.

with a flag or marker number. The finished sketch will usually be to a scale (e.g., 1/8 inch equals one foot for indoor scenes, and one inch equals twenty feet for outdoor scenes). A finished sketch may also become the basis for a model or mockup that the prosecutor may use in court.

### Processing the Crime Scene

The last step in the protocol is to process the crime scene for physical evidence for later analysis by a crime laboratory. In homicide and sexual assault cases, physical evidence is a major factor in determining guilt or innocence of a suspect.

Physical evidence, witnesses, and confessions are the holy trinity for solving major crimes. Despite Hollywood's portrayal, a crime scene investigation is not solved with

special effects. It is not that the science used is incorrect, but rather the timeline. Crime scene investigation is often a challenging and time-consuming effort. A crime scene investigator's job requires knowing some things intuitively, on-the-job experience, and the arbitrary distribution of events or outcomes, sometimes called luck.

The first systematic use of fingerprint identification began in the United States in 1902. The New York Civil Service Commission established the practice of fingerprinting applicants to prevent them from having a better qualified person take their tests for them. The growing need and demand by police officials for a national repository and clearing-house for fingerprint records led to an act of Congress on July 1, 1921, calling for the creation of the Identification Division of the FBI. In 1924, the FBI established the Identification Division to provide one central repository of fingerprints. In 1992, the Identification Division became the Criminal Justice Information Services (CJIS) Division. *FBI*

### TYPES OF EVIDENCE

Evidence used to resolve a crime may cover any of four areas of evidence: testimonial, physical, documentary, and demonstrative. Testimonial evidence is witness accounts of the incident or court testimony. Physical evidence refers to any material items that are present at the crime scene. Documentary evidence is usually any writing, sound, or video recording. Demonstrative

Detective Sergeant Ed Williams of the Morris County Sheriff's Criminal Investigation Section looks through a fingerprint file. The paper fingerprint file is useful in crimes that present the MO of a known individual. The crime scene prints can be compared to a suspect's ten (finger)-print card on file.

evidence is evidence used to illustrate, demonstrate, or re-create something tangible; for example, a room model mockup of the crime scene.

Evidence breaks down into two categories, class and individual, based on its characteristics and comparison value. Class identification would be, for example, a footwear impression that does not have enough characteristics to be individual but is the same size, shape, and design. Individual identifications are, for example, a fingerprint; a tire or tool impression could be individual if they have enough characteristics. Blood could also be individual if it is identified via DNA to one person.

"It is important to be able to recognize what should be present at a crime scene but is not, such as the victim's vehicle, wallet, or jewelry," said one investigator. "Also, objects which appear to be out of place, such as a ski mask that may have been left by the assailant." Although there are common items that are frequently collected as evidence—fingerprints, shoe prints, or bloodstains—literally any object can be physical evidence. "Anything which can connect a victim to a suspect, or a suspect to a victim, or crime scene is relevant physical evidence," he said.

This FBI evidence response technician sketches the crime scene to scale. Sketches are sometimes presented in court to supplement photographs and video.

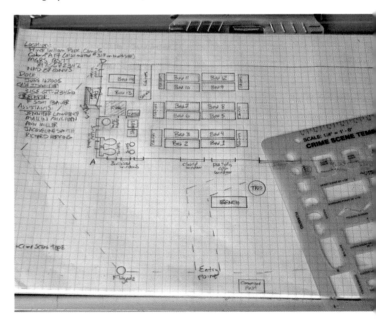

Sketches of a crime scene may be done with preformed templates of commonly used items.

A fingerprint is either a 100 percent match or not a match. There is no in between. Because prints are unique to each individual, even the slightest difference between any two prints means there simply is no match.

Impressed prints are not transfers but actual physical moldings of a set of friction ridges. Wax, gum, caulk or putty around windows, and almost any malleable surface have the potential to contain print impressions.

A single footprint may be matched to a single piece of footwear. The distance between prints indicates the height of the individual. The position of the feet on the floor indicates how the individual moved. Depending on whether the individual is running, standing, or creeping, different parts of the foot strike the surface in different ways.

The transfer of a fingerprint from one surface to another is rare and difficult. The print would have to have enough oil or moisture for a successful transfer. If a print is transferred, the fingerprint examiner would not ordinarily know it was a transfer and would get a reverse print upon lifting, one that would not be readily identifiable to a suspect.

Trace evidence includes gunshot residue (GSR), arson accelerants, paint, glass, fibers, and more.

The chain of custody establishes:

- Who had contact with the evidence
- The date and time the evidence was handled
- The circumstances for the evidence being handled
- What changes, if any, were made in the evidence

Detective Bruce Dunn of the Morris County Sheriff's Criminal Investigation Section holds an evidence scale next to pry marks he plans to photograph at a burglary and theft crime scene. The identification of the screwdriver used to pry open a door may seem mundane when compared to the identification of a homicide bullet, but it can be just as important in the prosecution of criminal cases. Dunn's crime scene photographs will include overall shots of the building, points of entry and exit, pry or tool marks, areas disturbed, evidence collected, and latent prints without ruler and with ruler for a 1:1 reproduction.

## CHAIN OF CUSTODY

The important chain of custody for the evidence at a crime scene usually starts with the collection done by the crime scene investigator. The chain of custody is defined as the witnessed, written record of all of the individuals who maintained unbroken control over the items of evidence. Chain of custody documents should include the name of the individual collecting the evidence, each person or entity subsequently having custody of it, dates the items were collected or transferred, the agency and case number, victim's or suspect's name, and a brief description of the item. The chain of custody establishes the proof that the items of evidence collected at the crime scene are the same evidence being presented in court.

## COLLECTING EVIDENCE

In law enforcement, it is axiomatic that physical evidence can never be overdocumented or overcollected. For major crime scenes, marking evidence occurs when the object is declared to be potential evidence. Marking is usually done with a numerical card or with a flag.

Collection occurs when all the evidence has been marked, photographed, and sketched. Initially, the evidence will be without context. It is the investigator's job to put the evidence in the context of the crime. Plastic containers (for liquids), new (from the manufacturer) brown paper evidence bags, or, in the case of large pieces of evidence, special cardboard boxes, are the general containers for collecting evidence.

Fragile evidence is collected right after being photographed. Vacuums are used indoors for fiber, dirt, glass, and hair. For an outdoor scene, soil is collected under the body and up to one hundred yards from the immediate scene. Surface soil samples may be collected using footwear or large fingerprint lifters, in addition to a few tablespoons taken three to four inches deep.

While laboratory analysis cannot give a positive identification of the soil coming from a specific source (except in a few circumstances), it can give the investigator probable cause to look further and it can eliminate other sources.

Automotive carpet fibers are frequently found in abduction and homicide cases when victims were transported in vehicles. The FBI Laboratory's Trace Evidence Unit can determine the make, model, and year of vehicles on the basis of physical, optical, and chemical information searches of the Automotive Carpet Fiber Database.

Evidence discovered outdoors must be marked and a flag added to warn others not to trample over the evidence.

Bloody razor blades found at a homicide are likely the murder weapons used to cut the victim's throat. On top of functioning as a natural ink, blood can also become a perfect substance for picking up impression prints. DNA analysis will reveal if it is the victim's blood; however, the killer may have cut himself on the blade during the act, and his DNA may also be discovered. Whole blood and semen, when collected and preserved properly, will virtually always yield a complete DNA profile. "When the evidence indicates a murder was personal, such as close-up multiple stab wounds, a person's throat was cut, or where the killer covered the body, we start with the people closest to the victim and work out from there," said one investigator. *Morris County Sheriff's Office*

Large evidence is firmly secured in a box and clearly marked, identifying the item, the date it was collected, the location, and the investigator who packaged the evidence. It is then sealed with evidence tape, logged, and shipped to the laboratory for analysis. Packaging the evidence in containers protects the contents from contamination and natural decay, and helps prove the evidence was not deliberately removed, added to, or altered. The containers are sealed in such a way that any tampering is obvious.

Tool marks that appear on horizontal surfaces such as window frames may be cast by applying compounds such as black Mikrosil to them. These casts are often called "popsicles" since they are mixed and applied with Popsicle sticks. The Popsicle stick may be left in the cast and used to identify the evidence.

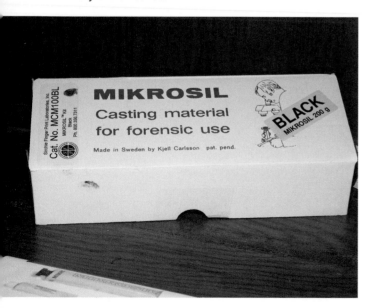

Casting materials like Mikrosil provide excellent small details and high contrast for microscopic examination. Mikrosil comes in various colors; black and white are generally used to lift dusted latent prints from rough or textured surfaces and impression prints in putty or clay, where regular lift tape will fail.

Plaster (falling into disuse) or dental stone (preferred) is used for foot impressions, tire tracks, or other impressions, which will not last on a surface. Fingerprints, shell casings, firearms, bodily fluids, bite marks, and tool marks all have specific methods of collection.

Trace evidence is never removed from any object; the whole object is photographed, tagged, rephotographed, and packaged. Two or more similar objects will go in separate bags, even though they are similar. Victim evidence is stored separately from suspect evidence. Bloodstained material is air-dried and placed in separate packaging that can breathe. The material should be stored in an area with good ventilation. Charred debris should be placed in an airtight container to prevent evaporation of any accelerant residue.

There are various techniques to reveal, lift, and collect fingerprints including use of chemicals, powders, lasers, alternate light sources, and other physical means. In instances where a latent print has limited quality and quantity of detail, a fingerprint examiner may perform microscopic examinations in order to affect conclusive comparisons.

Crime scene investigation, in part, is based on the premise that nothing vanishes without a trace. This is true in violent crimes. A murderer can dispose of the victim's body and mop up the pools of blood, but without some commercial cleaning chemicals, some trace evidence will remain. Tiny particles of blood may cling to surfaces for years.

Investigators may spray a suspicious area with a chemical reagent. Hidden blood spatter patterns may help investigators locate the point of attack and even the type of weapon used (bullets, knives, and blunt objects make different patterns of blood spatter). Luminol will cause any blood traces to develop a greenish glow. Luminol is the main ingredient in the chemical reaction. The luminol spray detects the presence of the catalyst—iron in the hemoglobin—by presenting a greenish white glow. This reaction is called chemiluminescent. Investigators may use other chemiluminescent products. Fluorsine and an alternate light or ultraviolet light source work in a manner similar to luminol and produce a natural fluorescence.

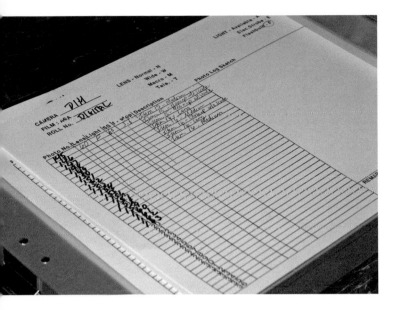

The photo log is an important part of the crime scene investigation and is necessary for possible later use in court. It documents the order and location of each photograph made. Information such as item description, f-stop setting, lens, shutter speed, lighting (flash) camera, film (or digital media), and the photographer's name should be part of the record.

If luminol or other chemicals, such as phenolphthalein, reveal apparent blood traces, investigators will photograph the trace patterns. Luminol only reveals if there is blood in an area. Other substances may be present that will give false positive reactions, so follow-up laboratory testing is essential. One of the newer field test kits, HemaTrace, reacts only to human blood.

Luminol produces a chemical reaction that can destroy nuclear DNA; however, it does not destroy mitochondrial DNA. For this reason, investigators may use luminol only after exploring other options.

## CRIME RECONSTRUCTION

Crime reconstruction involves the use of the scientific method, reasoning, sources of information on people, criminology, victimology, and experience or skill to interpret the events that surround the commission of the crime. A plausible theory of who, what, when, where, and why the crime happened should develop from information involving the victim, witnesses, crime scene evidence, suspects, interviewing, database searches, and other records.

Crime reconstruction typically starts with inductive reasoning and then proceeds to deductive reasoning. It involves an analysis of the facts. The number and kinds of facts, together with any ambiguity associated with them, determine the level of evidentiary value. The process is similar to the scientific method.

Step 1: Assert the problem; look at the type of crime and the characteristics of where the crime was committed.

Step 2: Determine a motive by forming a hypothesis from the physical evidence, interviews, and possible suspects.

Step 3: Collect the data; re-interview individuals and suspects, and take exemplars or comparison samples from suspects.

Step 4: Test the hypotheses. Evaluate how truthful or reliable the individual statements are, and compare the statements against the physical evidence.

Step 5: Follow up on the most promising theories with any procedures (e.g., surveillance, search warrants) that might establish or reject a particular suspect as the offender.

Step 6: Draw conclusions that demonstrate: the crime could have occurred in a certain way; or it likely happened in a certain way; or it was unlikely to have happened in a certain way; or it is not possible to demonstrate it happened in a certain way.

## TAKING NOTES

The crime scene investigator must prepare a permanent record relating the crime scene by writing a detailed report. This requires the skill and ability to observe small details of the scene and understand their meaning in relation to the evidence.

Interviewing or interrogating individuals is essential to discovering the truth, but a written record of all the relevant facts is equally important. The record must have all the known facts of the case, such as time, date, any witnesses, and the location and condition of the crime scene. Was it raining or snowing, clear or foggy? Was it daytime or twilight? Did the crime scene look fresh, or could the crime have been committed days or weeks ago?

Crime scene notes should contain as much detail as possible from signs of struggle, bullet holes, the description and location of physical evidence, any environmental factors, the disposition of the evidence, and all personnel who entered or left the crime scene area. "The scene will talk to you," said one investigator. "Make notes when things don't feel right."

"All crime scenes are based on the integrity of the crime scene investigator. The CSI has one thing going for him—credibility. It is like virginity; you only lose it once," said one instructor.

### PRETRIAL DISCOVERY

Parties may obtain discovery by one or more of the following methods: depositions upon oral examination or written questions; written interrogatories; production of documents or things; permission to enter upon land or other property, for inspection and other purposes; physical and mental examinations; and requests for admissions. Unless the court orders otherwise, the frequency of use of these methods is not limited.

Notes serve to refresh one's memory and may become part of the pretrial legal discovery process. Notes may qualify as *res gestae* evidence—circumstances and facts that may be admitted as evidence because they are relevant and shed light on the issues in question. For example, writing down an individual's spontaneous utterances may carry more weight in court as an exception to the hearsay rule and lend credibility to the crime scene investigator.

## RELEASING THE CRIME SCENE

Once all known evidence has been collected and packaged, and all other information has been gathered from the scene (photographs, videos, diagrams, and notes), a decision must be made to maintain or release the crime scene. The CSI should also make sure that there are no tools left behind that could lead to uncomfortable questions later. This decision will be based on an assessment by the lead investigator after reviewing the evidence collected and estimating the likelihood of anything else of evidentiary value being present. If there is doubt, the police will maintain the perimeter with an officer present to ensure its ongoing integrity. Once the decision has been made to release the scene, all equipment and reports are collected, and all evidence is transported to the evidence unit and/or crime lab. If a search warrant was issued, an inventory of items seized under authority of the warrant may be left at the scene and a copy may be placed in the case file. The crime scene release documentation should include the time and date of the release, to whom released, and by whom. Photographing the scene at this point will demonstrate later how the scene looks when it was released. Once the scene is released, re-entry may require a new search warrant if the original warrant has expired.

Approximately two-thirds of all homicides in the United States are cleared within the year committed.

## THE BODY AS EVIDENCE

The most important piece of evidence in a homicide is the body, and it requires special attention. Crime scene investigators are only allowed to make nonintrusive examinations and sketches of the remains. Examples of nonintrusive exams include: checking for identification, looking in the eyes, smelling for odors, and superficial examination of

Gunshot residue (GSR) is the cloud of vapors and particulates resulting from a controlled explosion within a gun. It consists of submicroscopic chemical particles deposited on the shooter's hand, face, clothing, or hair during the discharge of a firearm. Finding it on a suspect means one of three things: they fired a weapon, they were present when a weapon was fired, or they recently handled a weapon. For example, in the case of an apparent suicide involving a handgun, a gunshot residue test should be done on the hands of the deceased. If no residue is found, the case could be a homicide made to look like a suicide. If GSR is found, to protect the residue until lab examination, the CSI will put brown paper bags (never plastic bags) on the suspected shooter's hands and tape them around the wrist. There are commercial GSR identification kits that enable a CSI to field-test an individual for GSR.

A body found in a fire in a fetal position was probably alive and trying to escape the flames when the smoke overcame the victim. Bodies found in other positions suggest the individual may have been the victim of foul play and was dead before the fire started.

This fresh stain, found on the jeans of a suspect, appears to be blood and appears to have been left by the suspect wiping his hands off on his jeans. A presumptive test revealed it was blood, and later laboratory tests concluded it was human blood. The next step is to determine if it is the victim's blood or the suspect's blood.

wounds and injuries. The coroner or medical examiner is responsible for the body and everything that is on the body. They are the only person usually allowed to examine the body more extensively and make intrusive exams, such as recording body temperature. Before the body is moved, paper bags are put over the hands to protect any trace evidence under the fingernails. The body is usually wrapped in a white sheet (to preserve evidence) and is then placed in a clean body bag for shipment to a refrigerated storage facility, such as a morgue, for autopsy. A CSI will usually go to the morgue to photograph the victim in detail and assist with the removal of evidence.

### IDENTIFYING THE VICTIM

Often, the victim may not have a wallet or other identification, and forensic scientists use other methods in attempting to identify the individual.

The administrative worksheet documents major events, times, and movements relating to a crime scene search effort. Documentation of initial and continuing management and administrative steps ensures that an organized search is accomplished.

Although a pistol found at a crime scene may not have been used in the commission of the crime, it is evidence, and its processing may lead to the identity of either a victim or offender. This .38-caliber revolver looks clean and may likely yield fingerprints. Leaves and debris should never be removed for a better shot of the evidence. The evidence is first photographed in situ and then with a scale, since the scale may hide details that may later prove significant.

During the autopsy, the pathologist cuts away the crown of the skull, allowing him to remove the brain. In this case, the steel nail that punctured the victim's skull and killed him is now visible. *Morris County Sheriff's Office*

Fingerprints define each individual precisely. No two persons have exactly the same arrangement of ridge characteristics, and the patterns of any one individual remain unchanged throughout life. Fingerprints cannot be borrowed, stolen, or forgotten. They are not replicated, even in identical twins. Fingerprints offer an infallible means of personal identification. If the individual's prints are on file, either through civilian or military employment, or because of a prior criminal act, they will be used to identify the victim.

Dental records are also unique. The placement of fillings, crowns, and other dental work is unique to the individual, and obtaining dental records will confirm a victim's identity with certainty, but it is the job of the forensic odontologist in the laboratory to accomplish this.

DNA evidence is the most accurate means of identifying an individual, and it is also a function of the crime laboratory. "We tell our detectives that there is DNA in saliva. It is actually in the cheek skin cells found in the saliva," said one investigator. "There are many potential sources of DNA at a scene. Anything that touched the skin—for example, clothing and eyeglasses. Baseball caps are an excellent source, as the hat rubs against the forehead, pulling many skins cells onto the hat. Cigarette butts from a suspect's house are another source, as well as hairbrushes. Hairbrushes have the potential to yield both nuclear and mitochondrial DNA. Since DNA is a comparison test, a known sample from the victim collected at autopsy is also analyzed and compared to the DNA profiles from the evidence."

## FORENSIC PATHOLOGY

Discovering the truth about a victim's death continues to the medical examiner's laboratory. Today's modern crime labs are filled with high-tech equipment for DNA analysis, toxicology, serology, and the detection of chemicals. Yet, forensic scientists still are challenged with the time, and sometimes the cause, of death.

**The murdered and cremated remains of Madeline Murray O'Hare, an atheist who successfully eliminated the use of Bible reading and prayer from schools, were identified through the serial number on her hip replacement prosthesis.**

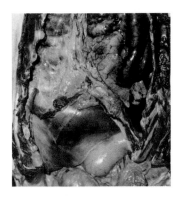

The autopsy of a body is just one part of a wider postmortem examination that includes identification of the body, photographing the entire exterior of the body, and possible X-ray examination. It is an opportunity to listen to the dead. Defensive wounds and other marks, such as lividity, often do not show up until the body is unclothed, and can shed light on the nature of the crime. *Morris County Sheriff's Office*

In postmortem investigations, a forensic pathologist performs the autopsy. The pathologist studies the effects of diseases, medical treatments, and injury on the human body. The pathologist's general focus is on soft tissue, including organs and body fluid analyses. The pathologist performs an autopsy to determine if a criminal act led to the death.

Human bone fragments were discovered in a fireplace by using an ultraviolet light. UV light causes the bones to glow.

There are several manners of death, and the forensic pathologist contributes valuable information about the circumstances surrounding the death. This information will help decide whether the death was natural, accidental, a homicide, a suicide, or undetermined, where there is insufficient evidence to reach a conclusion.

The pathologist will determine the cause of death assigned to the death certificate. This legal conclusion results from the analysis of the entire medical-legal investigation, including the crime scene investigation, autopsy, and toxicological findings.

## TIME SINCE DEATH

Estimating how long a victim has been dead is an inexact science. However, it is crucial to know when the crime was committed. If the investigator can determine approximately when the victim died, the information may help narrow the search for a suspect and eliminate innocent persons.

Traditionally, pathologists have used three stopwatches, or "the three *M*s of forensic pathology," which are still in use today—rigor mortis, algor mortis, and livor mortis—to determine time of death. The best known of the three, rigor mortis, begins about two hours after death. Rigor mortis is a stiffening of the body (hence the slang "stiff") that first becomes noticeable in the small muscles of the face and neck. It progresses through the body at a more or less specific rate, beginning about two or three hours after death, and then gradually disappears and is gone by hour forty-eight. Rigor mortis can be problematic as a gauge since it is influenced by disease and ambient temperature.

A forensic pathologist holds a doctor of medicine degree (MD), which requires a bachelor's degree with premed courses, four years of medical school, followed by a one- to two-year residency in pathology and then further training in forensic pathology.

Algor mortis is the slow cooling of a warm-blooded corpse as it equilibrates with the ambient temperature. If death occurred no more than a day or two ago, a pathologist can generally pin down the time since death to within a matter of hours. Contrary to what you may see on TV, no one can accurately predict time of death as precisely as 11: 15 p.m., for example.

In the first twenty-four hours, body temperature drop is the most reliable way to determine time of death. The method most often used is inserting a probe into the liver. The liver is the largest mass in the body and its core cools down slower than the rest of the body.

Liver temperature, relative to ambient temperature, determines an approximate time of death. Since the temperature of a dead body falls about one and a half degrees per hour, a 92.6-degree liver temperature indicates death about four hours before.

Livor mortis, or lividity, starts about six hours after death and is the postmortem purple-like discoloration of portions of the body caused by gravity pooling the blood in the lowest parts of the body. A victim lying on its back

**79**

will show lividity marks in the back, buttocks, and calves. However, lividity will not form where there is pressure from clothing or objects, and this can be used to determine if the person was clothed after death and possibly where the crime occurred.

Since the three stopwatches are only estimates, additional methods may determine more accurately the time of death. Within minutes of death, a thin film covers the eyes, and the eyeballs become soft. The gradual rise in potassium levels and an ophthalmoscope will reveal subtle changes for several hours.

Food in the victim's stomach will provide an important clue to the approximate time of the victim's last meal (within a few hours). For example, a light meal is digested in approximately one and one-half to two hours. A medium-size meal takes about three to four hours, and a large meal about four to six hours to be digested. It is a starting point where the victim was known to be alive and narrows the window of investigation. Investigators will attempt to locate where the victim had the last meal and possibly locate witnesses who saw the victim alive, perhaps in the company of an individual. The digestion of food follows a generally predictable timeline but can be problematic, and like the three stopwatches, digestion is limited in its predictability. Digestion is influenced by the type of food, any illness, drugs or alcohol in the system, the person's age, and body weight.

Crime scene investigators are encouraged to gather as much evidence as possible from a crime scene, but often the heavy lifting, the actual crime solution, comes from the crime laboratory or the pathology. When victims cannot speak, forensic science often provides their voices.

Barring a hit to the brain, the only way to force incapacitation is to cause sufficient blood loss so that the subject can no longer function, and that takes time. Tissue damage is the only instantaneous physical link to incapacitation. The critical element is penetration. The bullet must pass through a large, blood-bearing organ's center of mass and be of sufficient diameter to promote large tissue damage and rapid bleeding. Even if the heart is destroyed, there may be sufficient oxygen in the brain to support voluntary action for ten to fifteen seconds.

The only method of reliably stopping a human in a deadly weapon attack is to decrease the functioning capability of the central nervous system (CNS) and, specifically, the brain and cervical spinal cord. There are two ways to accomplish this: direct trauma to the CNS tissue, resulting in tissue destruction, or lack of oxygen to the brain caused by exsanguination and loss of blood pressure.

Physiologically, no caliber of bullet is certain to incapacitate an individual unless it strikes the brain. Psychologically, some individuals may be incapacitated by minor or small-caliber wounds. Those individuals who are stimulated by fear, adrenaline, drugs, alcohol, and/or sheer survival determination may not be incapacitated immediately, even if mortally wounded. A .22-caliber bullet penetrating the brain will cause immediate incapacitation in most cases.

A forensic pathology technician is a less technical position and may only require a high school diploma or the equivalent in some jurisdictions. The individual works closely with the forensic pathologist and assists with portions of an autopsy, sampling tissue, and drawing fluids from the remains. Job experience may count more than education, but having an educational background is a plus. The background requirements are generally a working knowledge of general medical laboratory procedures, medical tools and equipment, and understanding laboratory-safety and infection-control protocols.

The Criminal Justice Information System (CJIS) contains forty-one million subjects in the criminal fingerprint file and about forty million subjects in the civil and military fingerprint file. Each day, approximately seven thousand new individual records are added to the files. The CJIS provides ten-print identification services to all federal, state, and local criminal justice agencies, and authorized employment and licensing agencies.

## STAGES OF DECOMPOSITION

Decomposition consists of the processes of autolysis and putrefaction. Autolysis is the breakdown of complex proteins and carbohydrates into simpler chemical compounds. Putrefaction is the breakdown of tissues by bacteria.

A clinical autopsy is usually performed in hospitals by pathologists or the attending physician to determine a cause of death for research and study purposes. Autopsies such as these may also be performed at the request of the family of the deceased.

It is difficult to get fingerprints from most guns. Either the gun is well kept (too much oil) or not well kept (too dry). Any prints on the barrel are usually destroyed when the weapon is fired. "We get very few good prints from guns," said one investigator.

Latent prints are impressions invisible to the naked eye produced by oils and perspiration on the ridged skin on human fingers, palms, and soles of the feet. The uniqueness, permanence, and arrangement of the friction ridges allow examiners to match positively two prints and to determine whether an area of a friction ridge impression originated from one source to the exclusion of all others. Fingerprints can be recorded on a standard fingerprint card or can be scanned and transmitted digitally to a computer.

A bullet simply cannot knock a person down. If it had the energy to do so, then because of physics, an equal and opposite reaction would apply against the shooter and he too would be knocked over. The amount of energy deposited in the body by a large-caliber bullet is approximately equivalent to being hit with a baseball.

Possessing, threatening, or using a nuclear, biological, or chemical (NBC) weapon or material presents a de facto crime scene. The FBI is the lead law enforcement and investigative agency charged with responding to terrorist threats involving nuclear or other hazardous materials or weapons.

Morris County Sheriff's patch

Detective Tom Riedinger of the Morris County Sheriff's Criminal Investigation Section is processing a cigarette butt at a scene. Cigarettes are potentially viable evidence as they may contain skin cells from a person's lips or saliva. When multiple butts are found, each should be placed in a separate evidence bag.

Detective Al Dekler of the Morris County Sheriff's Criminal Investigation Section is taking a buccal (pronounced buckle) swab from an individual's mouth to acquire a DNA sample. The swab is longer than a regular Q-Tip, and the head of the swab is firmer than the head of a regular cotton swab. This enables the surface cells of the cheek to be rubbed off with ease. Investigators should always use clean disposable gloves when collecting evidence. Gloves should be changed when examining new items to avoid potential cross contamination of DNA.

Detective Dekler packages a buccal swab. Correct processing of DNA is critical to its use as evidence. Investigators should avoid coughing or sneezing near evidence, since their own DNA may contaminate the sample. It is important to handle evidence with care. Heat, humidity, mold, sunlight, and bacteria all have a direct effect on the integrity of the DNA sample and can degrade the sample to the point that it is unusable.

The immediate area within the tape is a radiological or hot zone where a simulated radiological device exploded, but it is not the entire crime scene. The crime scene extends out to where the last piece of bomb debris is found.

Drink containers often provide a rich source of DNA, especially if the user wore lipstick, where epithelial cells will be trapped.

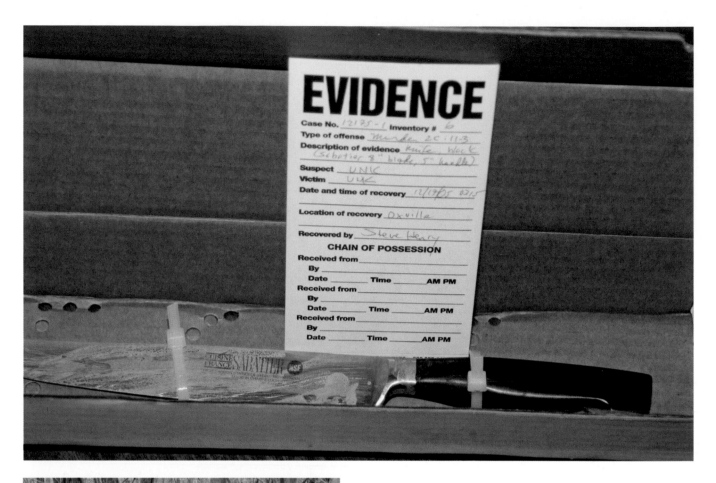

This large kitchen knife was recovered from a homicide. A presumptive test for blood revealed the dried material is blood, but it will take the lab to determine if it is human blood and if it belonged to the victim. The box will be sealed with the evidence sticker, and the chain of custody on the bottom of the sticker will be filled in as appropriate.

Detective Bruce Dunn removes the evidence in paper bags. Small evidence, except liquids, should be placed in new brown paper bags, which allow the evidence to breathe.

Body oils or moisture of some type are needed to form fingerprints. Costumes modeled from latex hand castings may leave impressions but never fingerprints.

Frozen bodies decay at different rates from bodies in dry or moist environments. The death timeline must account for these differing rates of decay. To make that possible, bodily decay is described in quantifiable terms. Even in the presence of external molds, bacteria, worms, and insects, bodies will decay from the inside out.

Deaths caused by injury, delayed complications of injuries, poisoning, infectious complications, foul play, or people who die without an attending physician must be investigated. The primary tool of this investigation is the forensic autopsy.

The medical examiner has legal jurisdiction of the body. The CSI should advise and work with the medical examiner.

The word "autopsy" comes from the Latin word *autopsia*, translated as "seeing for oneself."

Pathologically speaking, there are seven main causes of death: blunt force trauma, sharp force trauma, asphyxiation, gunshot, fire, drowning, and substance related.

# FOUR

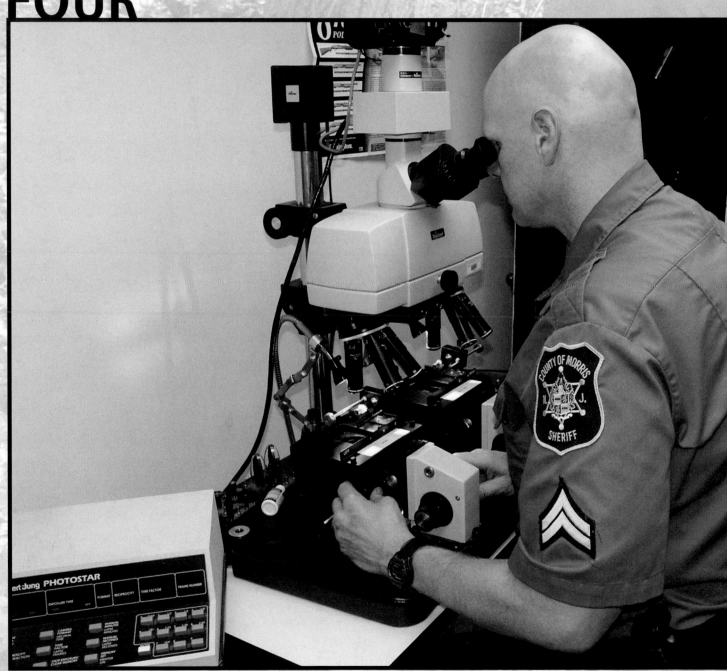

Detective Corporal Bill Stitt, a sixteen-year police veteran with thirteen years as a crime scene investigator, uses a comparison microscope to compare two bullets for a ballistic match.

# From Crime Lab to Closure

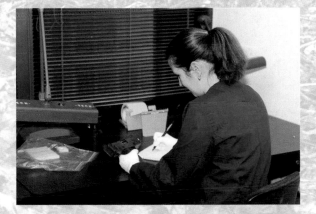

All evidence sent to a crime lab must be logged every time it moves to keep the chain of custody intact. This technician is logging in an automatic weapon. *FBI*

The crime laboratory is where the evidence gathered from a crime scene is analyzed in minute detail. Crime labs have existed for over a century, but it has only been in recent decades that they have become more sophisticated in the analysis of evidence and solving crimes. Crime laboratories now play a vital role in the criminal justice process. Scientific testimony is the deciding factor in the resolution of many criminal cases.

The FBI Laboratory in Quantico, Virginia, has the latest state-of-the art equipment. The laboratory's nearly 500,000-square-foot design has four floors for specialized laboratories and offices, and a library on the fifth floor. The facility is a model for security and evidence control with designated paths for the acceptance, circulation, and return of evidence. Laboratory areas are separated from offices and public areas to avoid evidence contamination. Access to examination areas is controlled with biovestibules to provide areas to change in or out of laboratory clothing and serve as airlocks between laboratories and offices.

Often evidence unseen by the human eye, such as fingerprints, DNA, samples of blood, and microscopic tool marks, can reveal the identity of both the victim and the offender. The results of the scientific analysis of blood, semen, fibers of clothing, hair, glass, paint, soil, bomb fragments, and tool or foot impressions left at the scene of a crime can be more compelling to a jury than the testimony of eyewitnesses. There may be five witnesses to the crime and, likely, there will be five versions of what they think they saw. With forensic evidence, there is only one version. "Physical evidence does not lie. It is what it is," said one investigator. "It is not influenced by emotion."

Forensic laboratories are usually grouped into specialties, which include the analysis of different types of evidence. Biological and chemical analysis, DNA,

The FBI Laboratory supports the federal and nonfederal criminal justice systems by conducting scientific analyses of physical evidence; providing specialized scientific and technical support to ongoing investigations; maintaining an automated database of DNA profiles from evidence and/or individuals for examination and comparison; providing expert testimony in court; developing a database and network software to match and exchange images of firearms evidence from violent crimes; and providing specialized forensic science training, analysis, and technical assistance to crime laboratory personnel and crime scene training to state and local law enforcement personnel.

The first crime laboratory opened in the United States in 1910. Today, there are more than 320 crime laboratories; the largest is the FBI crime laboratory in Quantico, Virginia, with nineteen departments.

DNA "fingerprinting" was discovered by British geneticist Alec Jeffreys in 1984.

ballistics, tool marks, computers, and questioned documents analysis are some specialized areas.

### BIOLOGICAL AND CHEMICAL ANALYSIS

Evidence associated with homicide, rape, burglary, and other crimes, along with fire accelerants and explosives related to arson and bombings, are analyzed for their chemical and/or biological composition. The results of each analysis may provide information that will connect the evidence to an offender, victim, crime scene, or the crime itself.

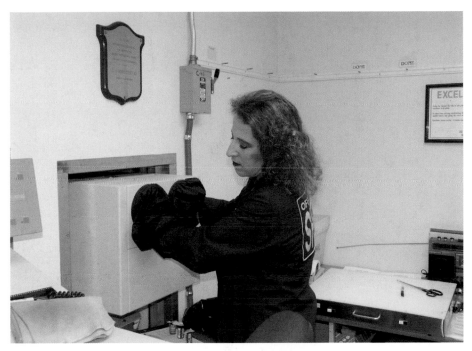

Fifteen-year veteran Virginia Walsh of the Morris County Sheriff's photo processing unit says, "We are currently using both film and digital cameras. We start each morning by turning on the photo processors and graphing or calibrating the chemicals." She removes the 35mm film from the cartridge for developing. This obviously has to be done in a no-light environment. "We make a contact print of the negatives and enlarge any the detectives want. The negatives and contact sheet of all the frames goes with the case papers," she said.

Twenty-year veteran Gary Colburn of the Morris County Sheriff's photo processing unit said, "Eventually we will go all digital when the other agencies are equipped."

Crime scene photos are submitted to the Morris County Sheriff's photo processing unit with any special instructions spelled out on the accompanying form. Only one roll of film is packaged in any request. Usually, the request for processing takes the form of a contact sheet (thirty-six frames printed on one 8x10 photo sheet). When the investigator reviews the contact sheet, he or she may ask for 8x10 prints of selected frames.

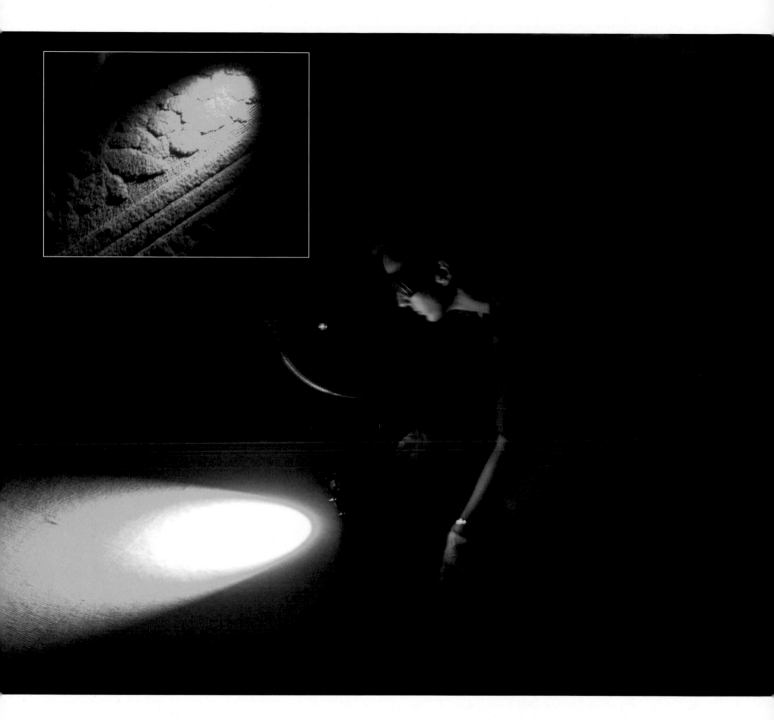

FBI Supervisory Special Agent Dayna Sepeck uses an alternate light source (ALS) to reveal latent forensic evidence (inset). Under an ALS and filter, the light stains of blood are revealed. Fluorsine is a chemical, which, if sprayed on the carpet, will reveal bloodstains under an ALS. The entire carpet on which these stains were found may be tagged, packaged, and sent to the lab for more detailed analysis and identification. Often, additional stains are discovered beneath the carpet on the bare floor. The agent uses a Mini-CrimeScope-400W, the most powerful crime scene forensic light source on the market. The specially designed 400-watt light may be set to various frequencies to detect fingerprints (on porous and nonporous surfaces), body fluids, human skin damage (bite marks and bruises), shoe prints, gunshot residue, human bone fragments, drugs, fibers, hair, paint, and grease. *FBI*

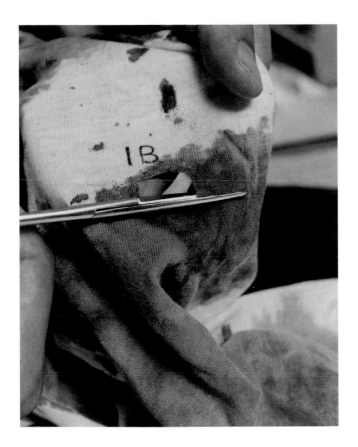

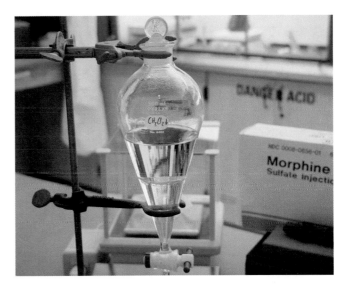

Crime laboratory work can be as dangerous as fieldwork. This container contains methylene chloride, which can cause irritation to the respiratory tract. It has a strong narcotic effect with symptoms of mental confusion, lightheadedness, fatigue, nausea, vomiting, and headache, and may cause formation of carbon monoxide in blood, which affects the cardiovascular system and central nervous system. *FBI*

This evidence may be bloodstained. Used for the presumptive identification of bloodstains, Hemident, commonly called McPhail's reagent, is nondestructive and enables the investigator to keep the evidence intact for further laboratory analysis. Each test is a compact, self-contained unit. The reagents are reliable and sensitive, and are capable of identifying one part per million of blood. Hemident was designed for field-test use and, as such, will not distinguish between human and animal blood. Laboratory serology analysis is necessary to determine whether the source is human or animal. *FBI*

The first biological attack in the United States occurred on September 25, 1984, in The Dalles, Oregon. The Rajneesh cult poisoned 751 people with salmonella in an attempt to influence local elections.

Lab technicians and crime scene investigators use a variety of tools to uncover trace evidence. Scanning electron microscopes can reveal surface details as small as one nanometer (one hundred thousand times smaller than a human hair). Comparison microscopes, polarizing light, alternate light sources, and the reflected ultraviolet imaging system are other tools for unmasking trace evidence.

A criminalist in a laboratory setting generally needs BA/BS in chemistry, biochemistry, biology, physics, geology, chemical engineering, forensic science, pharmacology, microbiology, molecular biology, immunology, entomology or criminalistics, or quantitative analysis.

Depending on the laboratory, biological analysis may be divided into two functions. The first identifies the biological materials. For example, is this dried dark stain human blood, animal blood, or something else? This is accomplished using a series of microscopic and chemical tests.

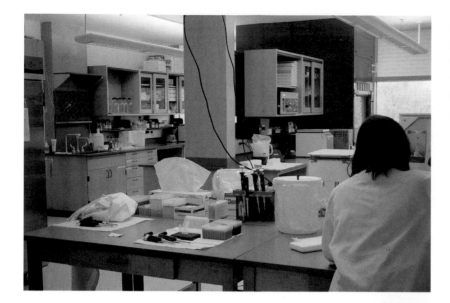

Many local law enforcement crime labs are understaffed, underfunded, and backlogged with evidence, and pressured to get results faster than ever before. In some crime labs, there is a several-month waiting list for DNA analysis. *FBI*

The second function is to identify the donor of the biological materials found at a crime scene. Is it the victim's blood on the knife blade, or is it the killer's blood from when he cut himself during the act of cutting the victim's throat? This is done by examining portions of the deoxyribonucleic acid (DNA), the cell's molecular fingerprint.

## DNA ANALYSIS

Finding blood at a crime scene has been useful since the discovery of the ABO blood group system in the early twentieth century. This kind of analysis, while limited compared to today's technology, allowed forensic investigators to narrow the suspect pool considerably. Now, however, DNA analysis is performed on the blood instead. The ability to identify conclusively an individual by their DNA is a quantum leap in the science of identification. The old system of typing genetic markers, such as the ABO blood group system, is not as comprehensive in the results as DNA analysis.

In 1901, immunologist and pathologist Karl Landsteiner demonstrated that there were at least three types of human blood, which he called A, B, and O, distinguished by the presence of antigens in the blood. A year later, he discovered the AB type and won a Nobel Prize. The discovery led to safe transfusions and a method of identifying and eliminating possible suspects through their blood types.

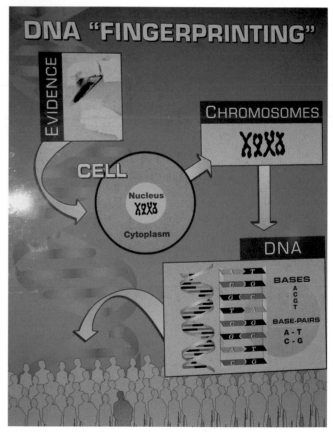

This chart illustrates how the evidence containing body fluids such as blood eventually reveals the donor of the DNA. One type of genetic material containing DNA is found in the nucleus of the cell (nDNA). An analysis will show that the odds of DNA being similar to another person are infinitesimal. *FBI*

This model, held by Detective Sergeant Ed Williams, illustrates the spatter of blood from a gunshot wound. The thin end of the droplet indicates the direction of the blood travel. Investigators then draw lines back toward the direction of origin. The point of convergence of these lines is the two-dimensional origin of the spatter. The point of origin lies at a point above the point of convergence. The investigator will then measure the length and width of the blood spatters and determine impact angle, which is equal to arc sin (width of the stain) divided by the length of stain. The more elongated the droplets, the greater the angle it came from. Measuring the impact angle will allow investigators to translate the two-dimensional convergence into a three-dimensional origin. Investigators then use a protractor to run strings from the blood spatter to each impact angle. The strings intersect at the origin of the blood shed, and the examiner can begin to determine the positions of both the victim and the assailant. Small lasers take the place of the strings, eliminating the need to tape strings to ceilings and walls.

DNA analysis is one of the most useful forensic tools in the crime laboratory. Other useful forensic tools include commercial preparations such as ABAcard, for the semen-specific protein P30 in semen stains, and kits for the identification of human or animal bloodstains.

DNA typing is more useful than fingerprints but more difficult to develop; the estimated probability of any two persons having the same fingerprint pattern is one in sixty-seven billion, or the equivalent of about ten Earth populations. The chances of a person having the same DNA (except for identical twins), is one in one

> Widely viewed as an almost infallible forensic science tool, DNA evidence is only as good as the individuals who collect, handle, and interpret it. Particularly, when DNA from more than one person is mixed in the same sample, which is often the case in sex crimes, analysis is an art as well as a science.

> Confronted with a possible fingerprint or DNA match, some defendants will plead guilty instead of risking a trial and the possibility of a heavier penalty.

hundred billion. The newest DNA analysis system, called short tandem repeat (STR), which is a DNA amplification technique, makes the odds of finding two persons with the same DNA approximately one in one trillion, or the equivalent of about one million Earth populations.

> In 1993, the bones of Czar Nicholas II of Russia, executed in the 1917 revolution, were tested and the mtDNA proved that Prince Phillip, husband of Queen Elizabeth II of England, is a direct descendent of the czar's sister-in-law.

> A search warrant may be required to obtain a suspect's DNA unless the sample is obtained from a public source, such as a discarded coffee cup, cigarette, napkin, or eating utensil.

DNA analysis requires only a small amount of material and can be performed on virtually any tissue since DNA is present in the cells of every living organism. There are two sources of DNA (one from the mother's egg and the other from the father's sperm) used in forensic analysis. Nuclear DNA (nDNA) is found in the forty-six chromosomes that inhabit the nucleus of almost every cell in the body. These chromosomes hold the bulk of genetic information that is inherited from parents. Saliva, semen, body tissues, and

**93**

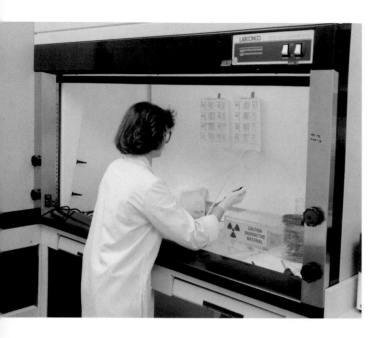

This lab technician performs a hybridization test. Hybridization is a method of identifying DNA with a specific individual. *FBI*

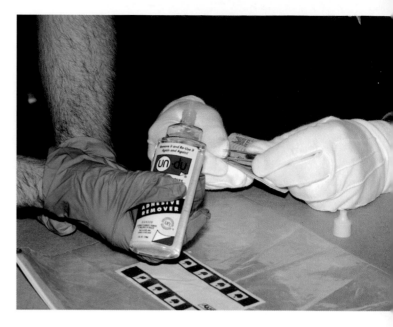

DNA is often found in saliva. A lab technician removes a postage stamp with a special adhesive remover so the stamp may be tested for DNA. *FBI*

hairs that have tissue at their root ends all contain nDNA. It is generally used to determine the paternity of an individual.

Mitochondrial DNA (mtDNA) resides outside the nucleus but within the cell and is typically analyzed in evidence containing naturally shed hair, bones, and teeth. There are only two copies of nDNA but about seventeen hundred copies of mtDNA found in one human cell. The mtDNA is passed on only along the maternal line. The mtDNA is especially useful with skeletal remains as it can determine the ethnicity of the victim.

DNA analysis is sensitive and complex; it requires particular skill and training on the part of the crime scene investigator who collects the biological material at the scene, as well as the individual who analyzes it in the

A recent FBI survey revealed that of all rapes, less than half were solved by the police, and in less than 10 percent of the cases was the DNA evidence sent to crime laboratories. Because crime laboratories do not work all cases submitted, in only 6 percent of the twenty-five thousand rape cases was the recovered DNA tested, leaving several thousand cases awaiting processing.

Crime labs must be nearly sterile environments, free from dust, dirt, and any contaminates that may influence testing. Crime labs must take precautions for their personnel. They are generally dealing with corrosive chemicals and aerosol sprays. Masks, gloves, eye protection, and other barriers are all means of protecting laboratory personnel. *FBI*

## USING DNA EVIDENCE

DNA profiles are used by criminal investigators to:
- Prove guilt: Matching DNA profiles can link a suspect to a crime or crime scene.
- Exonerate an innocent person: (According to The Innocence Project, 174 people, wrongly convicted, have been exonerated in postconviction DNA testing.) So far, DNA evidence has been almost as useful in excluding suspects; about 30 percent of DNA profile comparisons done by the FBI result in excluding someone as a suspect.
- Identify unknowns.
- Compare DNA profile to samples from families of missing persons to see if a match can be made. Even without a DNA match to conclusively identify a body, a profile is useful because it can provide important clues about the victim, such as his or her gender and race.

laboratory. Crime scene investigators must learn how to document, collect, package, and preserve DNA evidence. Coughing or sneezing on the part of the CSI collecting the evidence can contaminate the samples and make them inadmissible in court.

Body surfaces are covered with epithelial cells. These are tissues that form a thin protective layer on exposed bodily surfaces and form the lining of internal cavities, including ducts, glands, and vessels. These cells are continuously rubbing off and are sometimes transferred to objects (such as the offender or victim) with whom they

come into contact. Epithelial cells are a good source of DNA and are found in saliva, lick or bite marks, drink containers, envelopes, stamps, nasal mucus, and fingernails.

The identification and characterization of blood, saliva, semen, vaginal samples, and stains can implicate or eliminate a suspect. The information resulting from the examinations often assists investigators as they reconstruct the timeline of events that occurred during crimes, especially violent crimes against persons.

## MICROANALYSIS

Crime laboratory personnel, using microanalytical instrumentation, can identify and compare small particles and fibrous materials. For example, fibers, hair, soil, paint, glass, wood chips, building materials, vehicle head- and taillights, firearms, and tool mark examination all fall under microanalysis.

Trace evidence and unknown hairs found on this garment are collected by the crime scene investigator using a large palm-print lifter.

## FIREARMS/TOOL MARK ANALYSIS

Firearms comparison is a specialized area of the science of tool mark identification. Conventional firearms evidence comparison and laboratory examination consists of the identification of bullets and cartridge casings collected at scenes by crime scene investigators. This type of identification is as accurate in identifying a firearm used in a crime as fingerprints are in identifying a person.

When a firearm is used in a crime, there is evidence left everywhere. The bullet itself, the cartridge case, the partially burned gunpowder that sprays from the gun barrel, and the gaps in the gun's mechanism may all be found at the crime scene. There are tool marks on the cartridge case from the firing pin, ejector, breech face,

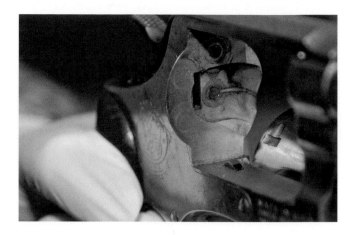

While the breach face of a firearm leaves impressions on the base of the bullet, the breach face on a revolver can leave telltale marks of the bullets in the cylinder, as the two impressions on the left illustrate. While this pistol needs a good cleaning, it is obvious how gunshot residue can blow back and get on the hands and face of the shooter. The dark spots on and around the breach face are some of the powder residue captured in the gun oil. Much of the residue easily escapes into the air.

The caliber of a bullet is the measure of the bore of the rifle or handgun in hundredths of an inch. A .44-caliber magnum pistol bore is 44/100th of an inch in diameter and takes .44-caliber ammunition. The magnum is not a measurement, but it describes the power of the propellant. A .45-caliber bullet and a .44 magnum bullet are similar in size, but the propellant is different. A .45-caliber weapon is not designed for the controlled explosion of a magnum load. The FBI publishes a book, *General Rifling Characteristics*, which contains the gun barrel characteristics on most weapons manufactured.

Tire prints can be as unique as fingerprints; each has specific characteristics. Syps, or small cuts, created in the tread of a tire during the mold process make each tire impression unique. The forensic technician rolls ink on the surface of a recovered tire, and then rolls the tire over a precut panel. The resulting track is in a black ink that dries immediately and does not require further development or protection. The panel can then be compared to a cast impression. Placing a coin between two treads will give an investigator something of known size, a scale to measure the depth of the tread. *FBI*

If a firearms examiner measures the spiraling groove engraved area (GEA) and the land engraved area (LEA), in addition to the number and direction (clockwise or counterclockwise) of the lands and grooves on a bullet, in combination with the caliber of a slug, the examiner can reference the *General Rifling Characteristics* handbook and determine the probable identity of a firearms model. The GEA and LEA produce a spiraling in the barrel to make the bullet spin, thereby giving it more accuracy.

The first recorded use of forensics firearms evidence was in 1879, when a man was charged with murder. A gunsmith's testimony that the firearm had not been used in over a year led to the man's acquittal.

## NIBIN

The National Integrated Ballistic Information Network (NIBIN) is a joint FBI-ATFE (Alcohol, Tobacco, Firearms, and Explosives) resource program that enables participating law enforcement agencies to store shooting-related data and test-fired exemplars from recovered firearms in one common system. It is capable of performing comparisons and producing probable matches or cold hits.

"Guns kill people," proclaims one organization. In reality, bullets kill people—bullets fired from guns by people. The chain of evidence is unbreakable. The bullet leaves a trail of information in its wake. Finding and interpreting that information is the basis for the science of ballistics. The bullet recovered from the victim can be precisely identified to the gun that fired it. From that gun, the evidence left on the gun can lead to the identification of the person who pulled the trigger.

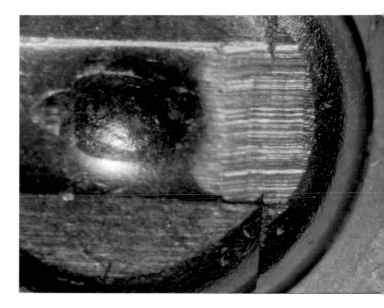

The comparison microscope presents two cartridge cases as one in a divided image. (The small notchlike mark in the upper right divides the images.) This makes it easy to see if the breech marks on both bullet cases are identical. In this image, they are identical. *Morris County Sheriff's Office*

Morris County Sheriff's Criminal Investigation Section Detectives Tom Riedinger (left) and James Rae cast a footwear impression. Casting a three-dimensional impression in soil, sand, or snow is necessary to capture detail for examination. Dental stone and water is used for casting most impressions. The casting material has sufficient weight and volume to erode or destroy detail if it is poured directly on top of the impression. The casting material is poured on the ground next to the impression, allowing it to flow into the impression.

Detective Sergeant Ed Williams fumes a Glock pistol for latent prints. Using cyanoacrylate (Super Glue) fuming to develop latent prints on objects has proven to be invaluable. The evidence on a nonporous surface is placed in a fuming chamber with a cup of hot water to raise the humidity. This, in effect, rehydrates the print. The cyanoacrylate product is opened and placed in the chamber. The fumes from the semiliquid adhesive react with the residues in the latent prints to produce visible white marks, which bond the print to the item. The resulting visible prints can be photographed and processed with powders or chemicals. This bonding, called "polymerization," allows the investigator to take more than one lift from the impression. Any container that can be sealed, such as a large plastic bag, may be substituted in the field.

and chamber. The breech face, on which the cartridge rests, has microscopic marks left by tooling used in the manufacturing processes, and these marks will be impressed into the base of the cartridge case when the gun is fired. If the weapon automatically ejects the cartridge, more unique microscopic marks are added to the cartridge.

Forensic firearms experts also examine firearms for operating features and defects to either include or exclude the weapon as evidence. Part of this examination includes function (the mechanics of the gun's mechanism are working properly) and accuracy tests, trigger pull measurements (the force required to fire the weapon), muzzle-to-target distance determinations, and serial number restorations.

Faces and other composite picture software contain a database of up to forty-four hundred facial features, including piercings, moles, scars, and tattoos, that allow a crime scene investigator to create a complete facial composite in minutes, which, once coded, may be exported to other agencies and used in police bulletins or on websites.

Drugfire is a national forensic firearms identification system that integrates cartridge cases, shotgun shells, and bullet analysis, as well as electronic firearms reference libraries on a single computer platform. Drugfire enables forensic firearms examiners to identify possible matches in microscopic marks on bullets and cartridge cases to determine if the ammunition specimens have been fired by the same weapon. With this information, examiners can link a firearm to one or more criminal acts.

In November 1998, a Pensacola, Florida, laboratory firearms section made a cold hit on Drugfire. It involved a 9mm semiautomatic pistol submitted by a county sheriff's office. The weapon was confiscated from an individual who was charged with weapons violation and aggravated battery of a police officer. A fired casing from the pistol matched an evidence casing recovered from a 1997 attempted murder. A victim was shot in the face while sitting in his vehicle. Prior to the Drugfire hit, the county sheriff's office had no suspect or leads in the attempted murder.

Crime scene investigators are trained to collect firearms and tools, as well as spent bullets and cartridge casings in a manner that does not damage any latent evidence. Improper collection and handling of firearms and cartridge cases can diminish their usefulness for identifying impression evidence and their admissibility in court.

A bullet goes through several steps in its manufacture. On the right is the lead slug. It is then covered with a metal jacket, and then the tip is cut away. Cuts are made and machined, making it a hollow-point round when it is finished, as on the left. The round in the back is a similar bullet that has been fired and expanded upon impact as designed.

Morris County Sheriff's Criminal Investigation Section Detective Kelley Shanaphy fires a Glock pistol into a bullet recovery box. Once the bullet is retrieved, it will be compared to the individual ballistic markings from a bullet recovered from a victim. The markings will either match unequivocally or not.

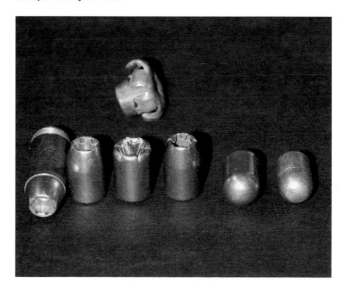

The bullets on the left are .38-caliber wad cutters used primarily for target shooting. They have a smaller grain (weight) lead slug and are loaded with a lighter powder charge. If fired into a human body, they would flatten out, but because of the lighter powder charge they may not penetrate enough tissue to cause serious bleeding (except for a head wound). The two bullets in the center are .30-caliber rifle bullets. They are semijacketed and designed to penetrate large animals such as deer and bear. The partial metal jacket will allow the round to travel deeper into the tissue before expanding. The two bullets on the right are .38-caliber hollow-point bullets similar to ammunition used by some law enforcement. The bullet is designed to flatten out quickly as it penetrates a body, causing maximum tissue damage and unconsciousness, or death from exsanguination. Law enforcement officers aim for the largest mass of the person, since this will cause the most tissue damage.

## THE SHANNON MELENDI CASE

It is rare that law enforcement can get a homicide conviction without a crime scene, body, or physical evidence, but with modern forensics, it does happen. On Saturday, March 26, 1994, 19-year-old Shannon Melendi, a scorekeeper at a softball game outside Atlanta and an Emory University sophomore, and 33-year-old Colvin "Butch" Hinton III, an umpire at the same game, left the ball field around 12:45 p.m. Shannon Melendi was never seen again, and her body has never been found.

Three days later, an unidentified man phoned the sex crimes unit of the DeKalb County Police

For an accurate ballistics comparison, all the examiner needs is a small portion of the bullet. Each of these fired bullets has enough lands and grooves on the base to provide a match if the gun is found. Drugfire is a computer database that stores images of fired bullet casings and bullets, either from a crime scene, from lab test firings, or manufacturers, and recovers possible matches for comparison by examiners.

Department, saying he had picked up Melendi from the gas station and still had her. Police traced the call back to the gas station, where they found one of two rings Melendi was wearing the day she was last seen. No further leads developed.

Although there are no fingerprints, no crime scene, and no body connecting Hinton to the abduction and murder, and no evidence as to the manner of her death, the state's strongest physical evidence came in the form of a small cloth bag that had specks of microscopic metal discovered by electron microscopes in 2003.

A forensic scientist testified to the specks of evidence. The scientist told the jurors that she found miniscule specks of rare metals on masking tape wrapped around a cloth bag containing Melendi's ring. She also found them on a roll of tape that investigators took from Hinton's car, and on several rolls of tape taken from Hinton's place of employment.

The presence of the metals on the sticky edges of all three samples of tape could only indicate one thing, the scientist said: "They [the different samples of tape] were from the same industrial environment."

Because Melendi's body has never been found, prosecutors sought to establish that the 19-year-old was killed by offering her banking and social security records, which showed almost all activity stopped in the weeks after she went missing.

The trial began on August 22, 2005, and ended September 19 after three days (nine hours) of jury deliberation. The verdict—guilty on malice murder and felony murder (the latter charge was brought because the kidnapping charge statute of limitations had expired). Hinton received a life sentence but will be eligible for parole in fourteen years. Both the Melendi family and the DeKalb County district attorney's office say that they will lobby the parole board to keep Hinton behind bars.

## FORENSIC TOXICOLOGY

Forensic toxicology is a specialty within analytical chemistry that uses a range of scientific analyses to identify and quantify foreign substances in a body. It reveals the harmful and often fatal effects of chemicals on living organisms. A forensic toxicologist will testify in court to the toxic or behavior-altering effects of a substance on a body.

A forensic toxicologist normally works with preserved samples of body fluids, stomach contents, and organ parts and attempts to detect and identify toxic or hazardous substances and unknown chemicals in the body. The toxicologist needs a thorough knowledge of human metabolism since substances seldom depart the body in the same chemical structure as they entered. The toxicologist will review the coroner's report, which may contain information on premortem signs and symptoms as well as the postmortem data.

Human hair is a good source of trace toxic residue. After ingesting a poison or heavy metal, such as arsenic, mercury, lead, or antimony, small amounts find their way to the hair root and, over a short period, are deposited along the hair strand. Since hair grows at a generally predictable rate, the toxicologist can determine when the poison was administered by its position in the hair strand. With a laboratory test called inductively coupled plasma mass spectrometry (ICP-MS), a technician can determine the type of poison. ICP-MS is a technique for identification of trace elements, and the test can identify almost the entire periodic table except the gaseous elements and carbon.

There are fifty to seventy-five plants in the human diet. The cell walls of these plants stay intact throughout most of the digestive process. Apples and potatoes have nearly the same cell wall, but a forensic endocrinologist or botanist can identify one from the other. After applying potassium iodine, the starch in the potato will turn black.

Poppy seeds contain trace amounts of opium, and eating foods with poppy seeds may cause a sample to screen false positive for opiates.

The first recorded reference to forensics comes from a book written in China in 1248. The book, called *Hsi Duan Yu (The Washing Away of Wrongs)*, explained how to tell the difference between a person who has drowned and a person who has been strangled.

Unlike synthetic fibers, hair is a natural element and picks up characteristics of the body to which it was formerly connected. An array of drugs and other substances are laid down in the shaft of the hair, making it possible to gather information that will or will not be consistent with known facts about particular individuals.

Contrary to the popular myth, hair and fingernails do not continue to grow after death; rather, the skin begins to recede. Hair is virtually indestructible, except when burned. It does not decay, so it will outlast the body and give useful information. Hair can be examined to determine human or animal remains. There are so many variations that only the work of an expert can determine which animal the hair comes from. Forensic scientists use hair samples to determine:

· Where on the body the hair came from; hair on different parts of the body has different cross-sections
· Race (sometimes)
· Some diseases

Napoleon Bonaparte's death in 1821 was attributed to stomach cancer. However, rumors persisted that he was poisoned. In 1960, forensic scientists analyzed a lock of Napoleon's hair taken from his head when he died. Their conclusion was that his body probably contained some fifteen parts per million of the poison; the maximum safe limit is only three parts per million. What remains unknown is if the poison was taken accidentally or administered deliberately.

This unknown liquid with a granular substance, found at a crime scene, had a foul odor but must wait for laboratory analysis to determine if it is evidence.

For certification as a toxicologist, an individual must possess a doctorate in one of the natural sciences. Undergraduate degrees must also be in these areas (biology or chemistry usually). Grandfather clauses may exist in some states for those without the mandatory degree level who have been working six years or more in the field.

Certification is bestowed by the American Board of Forensic Toxicology, and the expert may use the title of "diplomate," which must be renewed every three years. Board-certified toxicologists usually qualify as expert witnesses.

## FORENSIC ENTOMOLOGY

The crime scene investigator's main purpose, when insect infestation is found on human remains, is to properly document, collect, and preserve the insect evidence. The CSI's notes should include specific information regarding location of the body with respect to weather (rain, wind, cold or humidity) and the surrounding environment (woods, open field, etc.). A forensic entomologist in a laboratory does the actual forensic analysis of the infestation.

Forensic entomology has value in a death investigation, as it can determine when a death occurred. It can reduce the field of suspects and may help in identifying the victim with any reported missing persons during that

FBI Supervisory Special Agent Dayna Sepeck uses the Reflected Ultra Violet Imaging System (RUVIS), which intensifies UV reflectance instead of fluorescence as in other forensic light sources. The system can detect fingerprints on most nonporous surfaces prior to any treatment. The two main RUVIS applications are untreated prints on nonporous surfaces and cyanoacrylate-fumed prints. *FBI*

This is a bomb fragment that appears to be part of an electronic device and may offer the lab a valuable clue to the construction of the bomb.

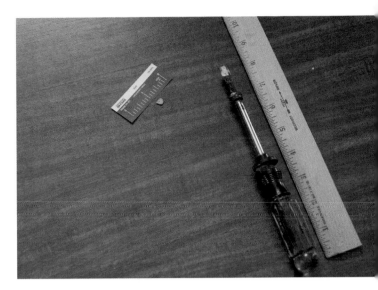

This screwdriver was used to jimmy a lock. In the process, the tip broke off. When the crime scene investigator found the tip, she photographed it next to a scale. Later, under a microscopic analysis in the lab, the tip was matched perfectly to the screwdriver.

· Airborne insects are collected around remains by placing sticky fly tape around the body.
· Egg and larvae (maggot) samples are placed in a solution of 75 percent alcohol and 25 percent water, which will kill them. Within ten to twelve hours, they should be transferred to a preservative of 70 to 80 percent ethyl alcohol.
· Live eggs and larvae should be placed in plastic containers with a damp paper towel.

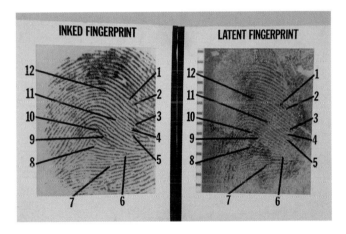

All the computer hardware and software do not take the crime scene investigator out of fingerprint comparison. Computers can narrow the search from millions of possibilities to a handful, but it still takes human eyes to make accurate comparisons.

The Anthropology Research Facility at the University of Tennessee Medical Center studies the processes and timetable of postmortem decay, primarily to improve medicine's ability to determine what is called "time since death." It is nicknamed the "body farm." Inside the two wooded acres, more than forty bodies lie in various stages of decay. Scientists watch the bodies closely to see what happens to them over time at the hands of nature and other disturbances. These observations help them learn how to interpret what crime scene investigators find in the field.

The forensic anthropologist position requires extensive educational preparation, up to a PhD, after which three years' experience in forensic anthropology is required before board certification in this field.

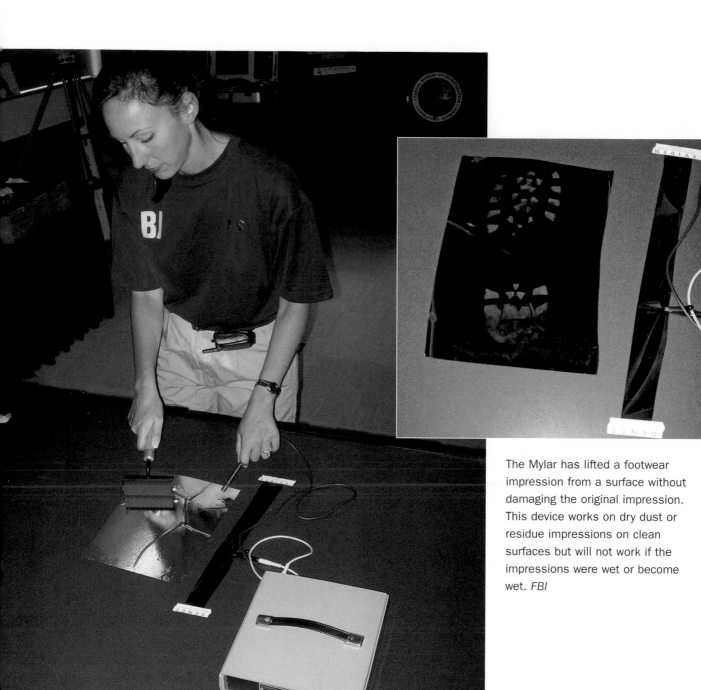

The Mylar has lifted a footwear impression from a surface without damaging the original impression. This device works on dry dust or residue impressions on clean surfaces but will not work if the impressions were wet or become wet. *FBI*

The electrostatic detection apparatus (ESDA) is a device that deploys an electrostatic field on a Mylar film to lift latent finger, footwear, and dust prints from various surface types. The surface of the plastic film has an electrostatic charge applied to it. The surface of the paper causes a different pattern of charging in those areas where there are impressions. Electrostatic impression lifts can be taken from most porous and nonporous dry surfaces. FBI Supervisory Special Agent Dayna Sepeck rolls Mylar paper on the impression. A sticky, transparent plastic film is placed across the ESDA trace to preserve it. *FBI*

time. Forensic entomology can also determine if the death occurred where the body was found, or elsewhere, by the type of insects common to that location.

## DOCUMENT ANALYSIS

Not all crimes are solved by collecting and analyzing insects, blood, DNA, fingerprints, or toxins. Sometimes a laboratory examination of documents will reveal evidence that will point to one individual or exclude another.

Documents retrieved from a crime scene may be examined to identify the writer or detect a forgery or alteration. The crimes may involve homicide, kidnapping, suicide, robbery, check or credit card forgeries, fraudulent insurance claims or medical prescriptions, extortion, obscene letters, forged passports, or driver's licenses.

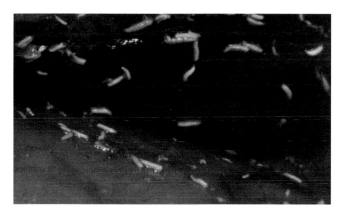

Of the millions of insect species, about one hundred scavenge on the corpse. A forensic entomologist must know the process of decomposition and the defined order of colonization of insects that infest the body at different stages of that process. If the body has been decomposing for a long period of time, the entomologist will determine the life stage of the insects collected on or near the body. Moments after death, the first organisms arrive. Most common is the bluebottle fly, also known as the blowfly. These flies enter the body through the nostrils, eyes, ears, and mouth, or, as in this photo, through a traumatized area of the body, the thigh. They lay eggs on day one, by day two the eggs hatch, and the maggots feed on the corpse for about five days. Around day six, the maggots pupate in the soil and around the body. By day twelve, the flies begin to emerge. They mate by day fifteen, lay eggs, and then die. The estimated time since death interval is determined by the development time of the species found at the scene. *Morris County Sheriff's Office*

The FBI was able to reconstruct several of the Unabomber's devices, but ultimately it was the bomber's brother who recognized the writing style of his brother, which led authorities to the bomber. *FBI*

A greedy daughter changed her mentally impaired father's will to gain more of his estate. When the father died, other members of the family became suspicious and called the police. The police investigated the cause of death—a fall down the stairs. They concluded it was not an accident. However, they needed to tie the murder back to the daughter. An individual's handwriting is unique, personal, and often hard to disguise. In this case, it was the signature on the will found in the home (also the crime scene). When compared to the victim's signature on canceled checks, the document analyzer concluded it was a forgery, and the daughter then confessed.

In the case of a suicide or ransom note, specially trained crime scene investigators or laboratory experts will examine the note to determine if the victim wrote the note under coercion, or if it was forged by the offender. The note is analyzed for the cursive handwriting or printing style. Spelling, linguistics in the note, and the placement of language—how the person worded the note, its syntax—are all valuable clues. The distinctive use of language patterns, simple and complex phrases, for example, and the distribution of conjunctions or adverbs may reveal a valuable clue if English is the writer's second language.

*Dear Sir,*

*Have 50,000$ redy 2500$ in 20$ bills 15000$ in 10$ bills and 10000$ in 5$ bills. After 2-4 days we will inform you when to deliver the mony. We warn you for making anyding or for notify the polise. The child is in gute care.*

Lindbergh Ransom Note
A re-creation of the first of twelve ransom notes demanding $50,000 (and escalating higher) for the return of the three-month-old baby Lindbergh that was found on the nursery windowsill of Charles and Ann Morrow Lindbergh's Hopewell, New Jersey, home. The placement of the dollar sign was European, and the basic lack of punctuation and grammar suggested that English was the author's second language, which was later proven to be a correct analysis. Notice, too, the characteristic skipping of the ink in some letters, common for fountain pens of the day. Law enforcement eventually caught Bruno Richard Hauptmann, a native of Saxony, Germany, when he passed some of the ransom money. Shortly after his apprehension, specimens of Hauptmann's handwriting were sent to the FBI Laboratory in Washington, DC. A comparison of the writing appearing on the ransom notes with that of the specimens disclosed remarkable similarities in inconspicuous, personal characteristics and writing habits, which resulted in a positive identification by the handwriting experts of the FBI Laboratory. Hauptmann was tried and convicted of murder, and executed.

## COMPUTER FORENSICS

Computer forensics involves state-of-the-art law enforcement techniques, particularly as crime scene investigations broaden to include the digital and wireless world of communications. Computer forensics is the application of computer analysis techniques to determine potential legal evidence.

"Often crime scenes involve computers," said one investigator. "Computers are used to commit crimes such as identity theft, hacking into private company databases, sending viruses, and terrorist threats," he said.

While most people use computers, few know how they work internally. Simply deleting data does not make it go away, and when computers are involved in a crime, the forensics computer technicians will perform bloodless surgery to reveal any hidden evidence of a crime.

It is possible to read the handwriting on the ashes of a note. Burned ink and pencil marks will reflect different wavelengths of infrared light.

Computer forensic specialists have a range of skills and methods for discovering data in a computer system or recovering deleted, encrypted, or damaged data. Any or all of this information may be useful during the process of discovery, depositions, or during the trial.

An individual rang the doorbell of his victim's home, fatally shot him five times in the face, and then set a computer in the victim's house on fire. The police brought the mound of melted plastic that was once a computer to the FBI Regional Computer Forensic Laboratory (RCFL) for examination. The examiners replaced the computer's melted circuit board with the same exact model. To add to the challenge, they had to retrieve a floppy disk that had become shaped like an S. After removing the casing, putting it into a new sleeve, and repeatedly cleaning the disk, it yielded the valuable digital evidence that the police needed to build their case.

Investigations into the September 11, 2001, terrorist attacks yielded about 125 terabytes of data recovered from various sources. The amount of data collected was many times the volume of information contained within the Library of Congress.

Some categories of computer crime include: child abuse (or exploitation through pornography); electronic stalking/harassment; gambling; smuggling; identity theft; counterfeiting; cellular phone cloning; telecommunications fraud; and software piracy.

"In the past, crime scene investigators would walk past a computer at the crime scene and look for hairs, fibers, and fingerprints," said the director of one of the FBI Regional Computer Forensic Laboratories. "Now we're seizing the computers and finding out a tremendous amount of information about the lives of the people involved."

It was not a fingerprint, blood spatter, or DNA that led authorities to a woman suspected of strangling a mother-to-be and cutting the baby from her womb. Law enforcement zeroed in on the killer by trolling computer records, examining online message boards, and most

important, tracing an Internet protocol (IP), the address or the unique number given to every Internet-connected computer, to a computer in the suspect's home.

Just before the slaying, the suspect had corresponded over the Internet with the victim about buying a dog from the victim. The same technology that makes instantaneous communication possible enabled authorities to crack the case in a matter of hours and rescue the premature baby alive.

## BOMB SCENE FORENSICS

"Every crime scene is unique. Approaching a crime scene where a building has been blown up is generally an overwhelming experience for personnel," said the chief of the FBI Explosives Unit. "We see physical devastation, the crime scene is scattered for hundreds of yards, if not farther, and we know there are probably victims."

A bomb needs an explosive main charge and some type of fuzing system. Fuzing systems can be either nonelectric, or electrical in makeup. Anything that can burn or create sufficient heat to ignite an explosive can serve as a nonelectric system. In the case of an electric system, four main components are required (a load, a conductive path, a power source, and an initiator). Finding the type of explosive used, the size of the bomb, where it was placed, and how it was transported to the scene are the first steps.

Large bomb scenes, especially outside, create immediate environmental issues. A rainstorm or heavy winds can alter the evidence quickly. Trying to dig out the important evidence before the scene degrades or is contaminated, without destroying more information, requires experienced eyes.

Bomb scene forensics begins with attempting to identify each of the bomb's components and trying to associate them with an individual or the group that bought the components and made them. Crime scene investigators who specialize in explosives forensics seek to determine, if possible, the bomber's signature—how

Human-scent evidence is, by its very nature, fragile and easy to compromise. However, there is technology that can reduce its fragility by using scent transfer units to transport the components of human scent onto sterile surgical pads.

Six test subjects handled four pipe bombs and two gas containers for one to two minutes. The explosives were detonated or burned, the debris was collected, and this evidence was processed by a scent transfer unit onto sterile surgical pads, which were then aged from two to sixteen days. Each bloodhound handler was then arbitrarily given a scent pad to present to a dog. The bomb handlers and six innocent decoys were sent out onto trails in an urban public park. The bloodhounds were placed at the start of a trail, given a good sniff of a scent pad, and used their specially trained "yes" or "no" response to signify a match or no match.

Overall, the dogs correctly identified the target person in fifty-three of the eighty bomb-debris experiments and thirty-one of the forty arson-debris experiments, with no false identifications. These are good results and support potential use in criminal investigations.

It is estimated that 70 percent of all terrorist attacks worldwide involve explosives. The FBI reports that of 3,163 bombing incidents in the United States in 1994, 77 percent were due to explosives. In these situations, 78 percent of all bombs were detonated or ignited. Another 22 percent failed to function as designed; only 4 percent were preceded by a warning or threat.

Between 1988 and 1997, there were 38,362 bombing incidents in the United States, an average of 4,262 per year, nearly 12 incidents every day, or 1 every two hours.

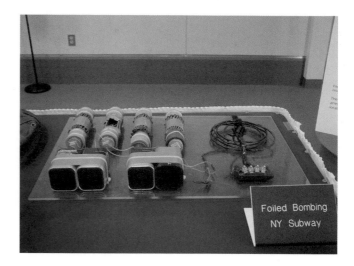

On July 31, 1997, a joint task force of New York City police and FBI special agents raided an apartment in Brooklyn, New York. Two men were shot and wounded as they were about to hit the detonator buttons on the five devices they had made. The pipe bombs are ringed with large nails designed to act as shrapnel and cause maximum damage to the human body. The recovered unexploded devices gave the FBI Laboratory an unprecedented look at the bombs and the terrorists. *FBI*

On July 27, 1996, a large bomb blew up in Centennial Olympic Park in Atlanta, Georgia. One person died, and more than one hundred were injured. The FBI Laboratory re-created the bomb from fragments of the exploded bomb. This was not a planned suicide bombing, since the FBI found fragments of a clock used as the timing device and a battery used as the detonating energy. *FBI*

On April 19, 1995, around 9:03 a.m., a massive bomb inside a rented truck exploded, destroying half of the nine-story Oklahoma City Murrah Federal Building, killing 168 people. Debris from the bomb was scattered over a twelve-block area, making it a large crime scene. FBI agents tracked down the bomber, Timothy McVeigh, through a truck rental agency after finding a vehicle identification number (VIN) in the bomb debris. McVeigh was later convicted of murder and executed. *FBI*

The soles on footwear bear unique characteristics based on wear and exchanged material. Footwear impressions are as unique as fingerprints, but the only conclusion that may be drawn from them is that a specific pair of shoes made the impression. It is still up to the crime scene investigator to put the suspect in those shoes at the crime scene. Similar conclusions may be made about tire marks.

the bomb was constructed, the design of the circuitry, materials used, including the explosives, and the method used to deliver the bomb. They will compare their evidence to others constructed similarly. They must also identify the evidence found with the bomb that is not part of the bomb.

At a bomb scene, it is not practical to collect every piece of evidence, so the FBI Explosives Unit acts as forensic advisors to local law enforcement or the FBI's

In the Oklahoma City bombing, the farthest fragments were about twelve blocks away from the epicenter of the blast.

A bomb does not destroy itself in the blast. Up to 95 percent of a bomb may survive the explosion, although it will be shattered into thousands of small pieces. Finding most of those pieces will often lead to solving the crime.

The terrorist bombing of the U.S. Navy's USS *Cole* blew bone fragments from one of the suicide bombers into an interior ceiling of the ship. The FBI Laboratory was able to match the DNA to an individual in a house in the city of Yemen.

An FBI examiner in the Explosives Unit, and two bloodhound handlers for two southern California law enforcement agencies, worked together to develop a new approach to identify bomb makers and arsonists through human-scent evidence recovered from postblast debris. Their study showed that human-scent evidence left by bomb handlers lasts and can be used to identify them even after undergoing the extreme mechanical and thermal effects of an explosion or burning.

The forensic odontologist deals with the branch of science that studies the teeth, their anatomy, the surrounding oral structures, their development, and diseases. If a forensic pathologist finds bite marks in a case of death associated with sexual assault, he or she may call a forensic odontologist to assist. The odontologist would make a photograph of the bite marks. Traces of saliva found around bite marks may assist in the identification of the offender (through the cheek cells found in the saliva). Lip prints found on various objects, such as around cups, glasses, or cigarettes, can often help in the identification of a suspect. A forensic odontologist must have a DDS or DMD degree, plus special training and experience.

A gas chromatograph can trace chemical composition and origin of materials in arson and explosion investigations.

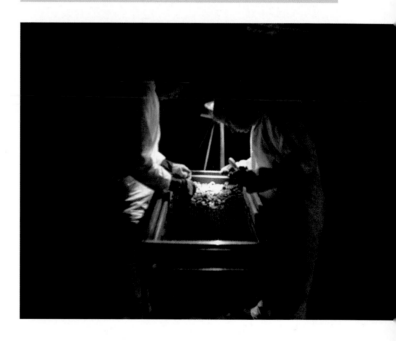

Crime scene investigators must collect the evidence where they find it, even if it means sifting through a scene in low-light conditions. They will often use sieves in progressively finer meshes to grade soil by particle size. Bomb debris is usually sifted through three mesh screens of increasing fineness, with the coarsest screen on top. Bomb fragments have a distinct look. They will generally have jagged edges and might be coated with residue or soot. *FBI*

evidence response team (ERT). It is best to grid the scene—divide it into small, manageable areas, assign personnel to small sections, and work outward from the impact. "We identify what to collect," said Greg Carl, the Chief of the FBI Explosives Unit. "We direct what evidence goes back to the laboratory, and in what order; we don't replace the ERT or local crime scene investigators."

It is a dynamic and sometimes overwhelming scene—broken and blown-out window glass, shattered office furniture, and victims, and amid this rubble are important clues to the bomb itself, and hopefully to the bomber, or at least who made the bomb. "We have to know what to exclude," Carl said. "You have to know how to build a bomb in order to know what to collect and

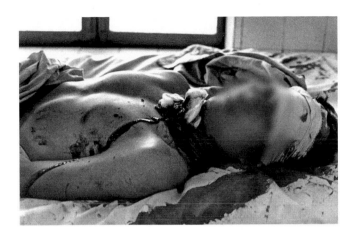

Imbedded in the body of a bomb victim may be important fragments of the bomb. *Defense Visual Information Center*

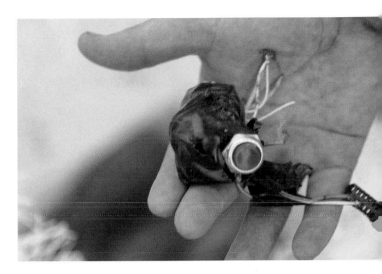

The construction of this trigger on a homemade explosive device revealed much about the bomb maker. It may also have the bomb maker's DNA. *Department of Defense*

FBI Explosives Unit patch

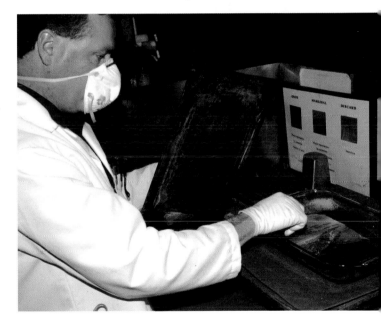

This technician is agitating a questioned document in a chemical solution to reveal latent evidence. *FBI*

what to exclude. We use our imagination to some degree, and ask, 'How would I build the bomb?' The more evidence we collect, the more information we develop in the laboratory. That's the key."

Because of the vast amount of debris in the blast area, the team leader must decide what is common in a zone. For example, there may be many blue plastic fragments in one area. Do they have some relevance to the bomb? They cannot bring back everything to the lab. "It is like looking for one needle in a stack of needles," Carl said.

Because a bomb scene is psychologically depressing, it is vital to decide what is important and leave what is not. "In the TWA Flight 800 scene, where the Boeing 747 exploded at 12,000 feet, we needed to recover as much of

**111**

Crime scene reconstruction is often vital to understanding what happened and why. The FBI re-created, to scale, the crime scene that was formerly the World Trade Center tower complex. *FBI*

This nighttime scene of a fatal hit-and-run left one person dead and enough physical evidence scattered around the scene for the crime scene investigators to later identify the vehicle. *Morris County Sheriff's Office*

FBI crime laboratory personnel provide forensic examinations, technical support, expert witness testimony, and training to federal, state, and local law enforcement agencies.

the airplane as possible. The wreckage was scattered over a wide area and was in deep water. It was dangerous work, but it had to be done to discover the truth," said Carl. "We needed to know what brought the airliner down. In the World Trade Center attack, we really did not need the airplane wreckage, but it was still psychologically important to collect it. In the terrorist attack of the USS *Cole,* we had the mental stability of the survivors to maintain. Interviewing them helped them cope with the devastation around them," said Carl.

At an outdoor bomb scene, the first priority is to prevent evidence contamination. "We photograph the scene for the record," said Carl. "We photograph everything again at the lab and do the analysis of the samples at the laboratory. We are looking for trace chemistry and, when possible, remains of the bomb so we can reconstruct the device.

"We found trace TNT, RDX, and bone fragments on the USS *Cole."* RDX is considered the most powerful and brisant of the military high explosives. "Later, we got a tip about a house in Yemen, and there we found DNA and RDX traces that matched what we found on the *Cole.* We also found fingernail clippings and mustache clippings, which was part of the bombers' ritual cleansing before their suicide attack."

The Latent Print Unit of the FBI provides training (on request) in all aspects of latent print work to local, state, federal, and foreign law enforcement personnel. In addition, the unit conducts research to evaluate new technologies, procedures, and equipment.

Forensic facial imaging provides composite drawings, two- and three-dimensional facial reconstructions from skeletal remains, facial age progressions, postmortem reconstructions, digital photographic manipulations/ retouches, and flyers with the suspect's picture and physical description.

Using a CAT scan, forensic scientists were able to make a precise model of the skull of the 3,300-year-old King Tut mummy. After further forensic study, they determined that he was five feet, six inches tall, had a slight build, was healthy, and was about 19 years old at the time of death. He had all his wisdom teeth; one was impacted, and none of his teeth had cavities. He likely died from an infected broken leg.

## HOMICIDES BY RELATIONSHIP AND WEAPON TYPE, 1990–2002 (U.S. BY PERCENTAGE)

| Assailant | Gun | Knife | Blunt Object | Force | Other |
|-----------|-----|-------|--------------|-------|-------|
| Husband | 70 | 25 | 2 | 1 | 2 |
| Ex-husband | 88 | 9 | 1 | 0 | 2 |
| Wife | 68 | 14 | 5 | 9 | 4 |
| Ex-wife | 78 | 12 | 2 | 6 | 2 |
| Boyfriend | 46 | 45 | 3 | 3 | 3 |
| Girlfriend | 57 | 19 | 5 | 14 | 5 |

## WORKING CONDITIONS

Some crime laboratory technicians and crime scene investigators may be exposed to hazards from toxic materials, equipment, or chemicals. Some personnel work with radioactive isotopes and nuclear material and may be exposed to radiation. Personnel may also work with disease-causing organisms. Other crime scene investigators are exposed to human body fluids and firearms. If proper safety procedures and clothing are used, however, these working conditions pose little risk.

Completion of the autopsy, laboratory analysis, and the associated death certificate may not be the end of the crime scene investigator's involvement in a criminal case. The case may go to trial months or years later. All or part of the crime scene team may be required to testify to the evidence, the facts of the case, such as the cause and manner of death, and perhaps give an opinion on a variety of questions relevant to the case. If the case does not go to trial because the offender cannot be identified or located, it will grow cold and may become the challenge of behavioral analysts.

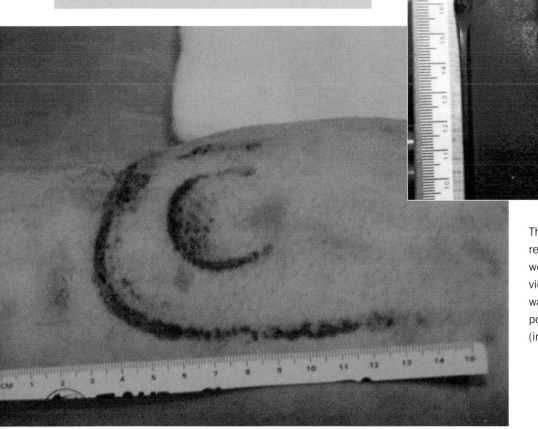

The postmortem on the victim revealed bruises on his left leg and would be the key to matching the victim to a vehicle. When the vehicle was recovered, the bruise matched a portion of the license plate holder (inset). *Morris County Sheriff's Office*

113

The vehicle was recovered on the street in front of the owner's house and impounded. It revealed significant damage to the right headlight area. It was clear that the victim was thrown into the windshield during contact with the vehicle. *Morris County Sheriff's Office*

The fracture line comparison matched the pieces to the vehicle, and the investigators arrested the driver. *Morris County Sheriff's Office*

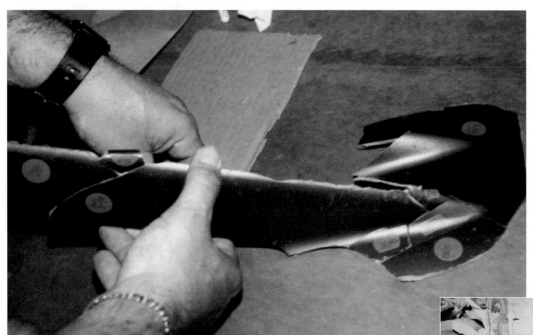

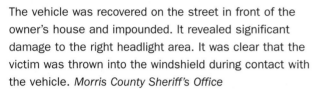

After the vehicle was recovered, the crime scene investigators began matching the pieces left on the roadway. *Morris County Sheriff's Office*

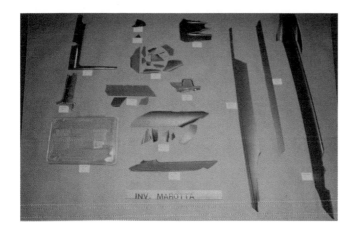

All the pieces recovered from the hit-and-run fatality are awaiting the crime scene investigator to piece them together much like a jigsaw puzzle. *Morris County Sheriff's Office*

One window of American Airlines Flight 11, which was flown into the north tower of the World Trade Center, was not needed for the crime scene investigation and placed in a place of reverence in the Intrepid Air, Sea, and Space Museum. The retired aircraft carrier housed over 700 FBI agents during the investigation.

Anthrax-laced letters sent to several politicians and media people became evidence and were sent to the FBI Laboratory for analysis. *FBI*

Deep at the bottom of Long Island Sound, navy divers found the suspected underwater crime scene of TWA Flight 800. Investigators later determined that the destruction of TWA Flight 800 was not a criminal act. *Defense Visual Information Center*

An alternate light source is one high-tech method of revealing latent prints. The light covers a range of frequencies, and, with the aid of an orange filter, can reveal prints or trace evidence unseen by the eye. *FBI*

The FBI National Crime Information Center (NCIC) 2000 is a nationwide information system dedicated to serving and supporting criminal justice agencies—local, state, and federal—in their mission to uphold the law and protect the public. NCIC 2000 serves criminal justice agencies in all fifty states, the District of Columbia, the Commonwealth of Puerto Rico, the U.S. Virgin Islands, and Canada, as well as federal agencies with law enforcement missions. It contains enhanced name search, fingerprint searches, probation/parole records, mug shots, convicted sex offender registry, and more. The unit maintains reference collections of human and animal hairs, natural and man-made textile fibers, fabrics, feathers, woods, and seeds.

Dental comparison of antemortem and postmortem records provides one avenue for establishing personal identification in the forensic sciences. Ideally, dentists work with antemortem dental X-rays, since these provide an X-ray image of a known person at a specific point in time. Comparing these X-rays with dental X-rays taken from unidentified remains may determine a match or exclusion. Usually, the sizes and shapes of fillings in the teeth can be matched to establish a positive identification. A computer program called OdontoSearch can create a means of using charts and notes (in the absence of X-rays) for identification purposes.

In 1999, the FBI developed and implemented a national automated fingerprint system known as the Integrated Automated Fingerprint Identification System (IAFIS). Although IAFIS is primarily a palm and ten-print system for searching an individual's fingerprints to determine whether a prior arrest record exists, it maintains a criminal arrest record history for each individual; the system also offers significant latent print capabilities. Using IAFIS, a latent print specialist can digitally capture latent print and ten-print images and perform several functions with each. These include:

- Enhancement to improve image quality
- Comparison of latent fingerprints against suspect ten-print records retrieved from IAFIS
- Searches of IAFIS when no suspects have been developed
- Automatic searches of new arrest ten-print records against an unsolved latent fingerprint repository
- Creation of special files of ten-print records in support of major criminal investigations

In June 2000, a male security guard was murdered. Then, during a robbery, two male store clerks were murdered. Firearms evidence was recovered from both scenes and submitted for examination. The .40-caliber bullets and cartridge cases were entered into the National Integrated Ballistic Information Network. The ballistics examination indicated that the same gun was used at both scenes. These cases were also linked with an aggravated robbery that occurred in May 2000. Further investigation linked an aggravated robbery that occurred in February 2000, when a wallet was stolen and a credit card used.

The physical presence of blood droplets, their shape and number, as well as the patterns made when they fell or were sprayed against walls, floor, or ceiling, tell a story. The pattern reveals the velocity of the droplets; the smaller the drops, the faster they were traveling. Blood drops are usually put in motion by a blow from an object or weapon, with blood pushed ahead of the item making the impact. A pattern of tiny droplets indicates high velocity, such as a gunshot or an explosive device. Large drops often indicate low-impact injuries such as a punch. Midsize droplets almost always suggest a knife or blunt object impact.

Toxins are poisonous substances produced by an animal, plant, or microbe. They differ from toxic chemical agents in that they are not man-made and are typically more complex materials.

**MEDICAL MAXIM**

- The psychiatrist knows nothing and does nothing.
- The surgeon knows nothing and does everything.
- The pathologist knows everything but is always a day too late.

# FIVE

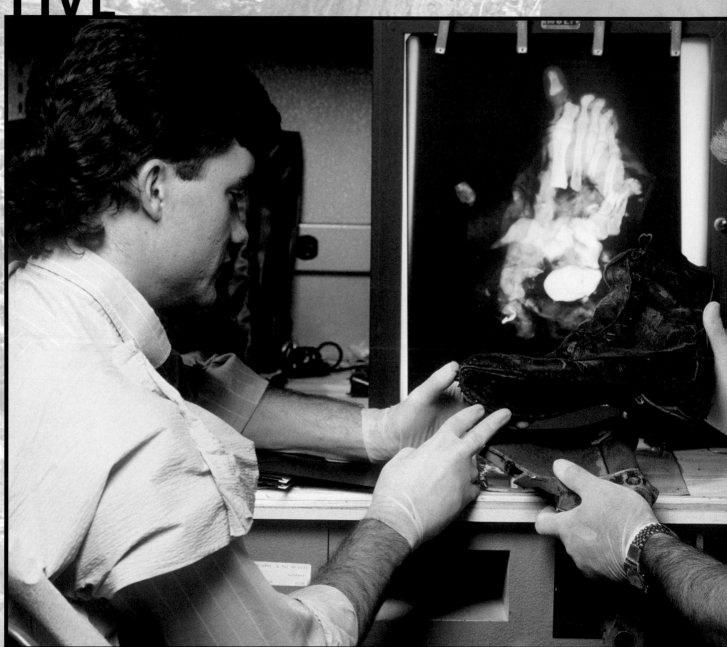

Investigators study a boot and compare it to the X-ray in the background. *Defense Visual Information Center*

# Serial Crimes

At a recovery site, the anthropologist directs the excavation. Each mission is unique, but there are certain things that each recovery has in common. The first step is for the anthropologist to define the site or determine the site perimeter. Once that has been defined, a grid system is established. Careful excavation occurs using that grid system. Every inch of soil that comes out of the site is screened for any potential remains or personal effects. Initial analysis occurs at the site, and the materials or remains are delivered to the lab for further examination. The first questions to be answered are who is the victim, and are the remains those of a serial victim or a random crime of opportunity? *FBI*

No one knows exactly what drives someone to commit serial rape and murder. The motive for any criminal act can be spontaneous and simple, or planned and complex, and it may not always be as it first appears. We are used to explaining murder in terms of greed, jealousy, profit, or passion, but serial killers are different from other killers. They have a compulsion to kill. Some say it is a genetic defect, others say it is because of deviant or dysfunctional experiences in their childhood. Still others speculate that the serial killer kills for atavistic pleasure, the result of a throwback or reappearance of an individual trait after several generations of absence. Serial killers are cowards who usually target those who cannot always defend themselves: women and children. They derive a sexual satisfaction from the power over life and death, the killing, or the events leading up to the killing.

These human remains, although only partially uncovered, will be wrapped in a white body bag (near the head of the victim) and taken to the medical examiner for autopsy. *FBI*

Investigators dig up the remains of a murdered individual. The arms and shoulders are just visible as one investigator begins to remove the dirt around the victim's head. Note the duct tape sealing the gloves to the investigator's sleeve to prevent contamination. Estimation of time since death of skeletal human remains is an important issue in forensic anthropology. It usually is difficult to determine from morphological information alone if skeletal remains represent a postmortem interval of several or many years. Often, evidence beneath the corpse, such as cigarette butts or condoms, discarded by the offender will provide valuable evidence. *FBI*

As of this writing, there are at least fifteen hundred serial killers on record and many more than that number of their victims of unsolved crimes. At any given time, there are estimated to be twenty to fifty active serial killers, and those who change their targets or methods are often never identified. Solving many of these serial crimes is difficult, and if they are solved, it is not until years later. These crimes usually become cold cases and are not reopened unless there is a confession, DNA identification, or new physical evidence.

The FBI Behavioral Analysis Unit (BAU), part of the National Center for the Analysis of Violent Crime (NCAVC) at Quantico, Virginia, responds to law enforcement's unusual, vicious, and emotionally charged serial crimes. Typically, they are involved in terror threat assessment; crimes against children, such as abductions, molestations, and child homicides; crimes against adults, such as serial rapes and murders; "overkilled" (multiple stabbing) victims; and dismemberments.

In serial offender cases, the FBI behavioral analysts balance three conflicting forces: the public's right to know, law enforcement's desire to manage information to maintain case integrity and public safety, and the media's need to run stories and compete in their markets.

The FBI Behavioral Science Unit (BSU) at Quantico, Virginia, provides programs of training, research, and consultation in the behavioral and social sciences in support of the law enforcement and intelligence communities' operational effectiveness. It focuses on developing new and innovative investigative approaches and techniques in the solution of crime by studying the offender and his or her behavior and motivation.

To obtain a conviction, police generally need a confession, irrefutable forensic evidence, consistent eyewitness accounts, or strong circumstantial evidence. Behavioral analysis gives law enforcement a relatively new and powerful tool in that regard. Supervisory special agents assigned to the NCAVC perform the tasks commonly associated with profiling; however, the FBI does not have a job title called profiler.

A profile is a description of the traits and characteristics of an unknown subject (UNSUB) in a specific case. A criminal profile is created when there is insufficient forensic evidence to solve a vicious and seemingly motiveless crime. Generally, the profile of an UNSUB will reduce the suspect population. Criminal profiling, behavioral profiling, offender profiling, or just profiling, are names for the behavioral analysis techniques. Profiling did not always have a sinister connotation, but it now suggests an individual is singled out because of his or her race, which is unsatisfactory and contrary to acceptable police procedures. The profiling done at the NCAVC identifies behavioral traits of an unknown offender, and has nothing to do with racial profiling.

A behavioral analyst attempts to assess the criminal act, interpret offender behavior, and/or interact with the victim for the purposes of providing crime analysis, investigative suggestions, profiles of unknown offenders, threat analysis, and expert testimony.

Geographic profiling is an investigative aid that predicts a violent serial offender's most likely location, including home, work, social venues, and travel routes. Information from a series of related crimes is input into a mathematical model that analyzes the locations of the crimes and the characteristics of the local neighborhoods. The computer produces a map showing the areas in which the offender most likely lives and works. Geographic profiling is useful in serial crime when the offender is unknown. A minimum of five crimes or related sites are required for a complete profile, but some form of analysis can be done with less information.

## BEHAVIORAL ANALYSIS

In the late 1950s, psychiatrist James Brussell developed the first modern criminal profile of New York City's "Mad Bomber," George Metesky, who was responsible for more than thirty bombings. In 1969, FBI Special Agent Howard Teten, later joined by Pat Mullaney at the FBI National Academy, began applying and refining the techniques that Brussell pioneered. Teten was teaching a course on applied criminology, and law enforcement personnel would bring their unsolved homicide cases to the course. As the classes discussed the cases, patterns of criminal behavior began to emerge. Teten began to see some crime scene patterns fit certain mental disorders; among them was one called simple schizophrenia (later called undifferentiated schizophrenia), an illness that develops at puberty. With further study, Teten and others began to discover how the serial offender's behavior changed with his age, and the offender's age could be estimated based on the type of crime he commits. In 1978, after Teten left the Behavioral Science Unit, John Douglas and Robert Ressler modified the process to categorize the organized and disorganized offender, which is in use today.

Serial crime investigators will draw conclusions from patterns that emerge by comparing crime scenes in hundreds of similar cases with the behavioral characteristics of the offenders apprehended in those cases. They will also interview the offender, if possible, for further insights. Contrary to the movie *The Silence of the Lambs*, which took dramatic license, the FBI never sends a new agent trainee to interview a subject. "We have two new people in the unit," said a senior agent, "and they each have more than ten years on the job."

Those who study criminal behavior generally use one of two approaches. The first, inductive reasoning, assumes that criminals will have backgrounds and motives similar to those of other serial criminals who have behaved the same way. Deductive reasoning, although still based on a degree of probability, avoids generalizations and averages. Instead, it studies the individual offender's actions before, during, and after the crime in great detail, and the investigator makes further deductions based on new evidence.

Behavioral analysts do not get psychic flashes at a crime scene. They live in a world of inductive and deductive reasoning. They use behavioral-based investigative techniques and apply their education, crime-solving experience, research, and knowledge of criminal behavior. They also factor in the facts and statistical probabilities to these complex and often time-sensitive crimes.

In its strictest sense, criminal justice profiling occurs when investigators strategically consider characteristics such as race, gender, religion, sexual orientation, age, and many other factors to make discretionary decisions in the course of their investigations.

Behavioral scientists study a wide variety of behaviors, both human and animal, to better understand the complex human behavior.

The forensic anthropologist must help identify the skeletal remains of the victim and determine whether the death was related to a crime. The first step is to find out if the bones are human. Bones of certain animals resemble a number of bones found in humans. For example, a horse's tailbones look similar to human finger bones. These bones, found in a remote wooded area, at first looked similar to a small child's bones, but they turned out to be those of a newborn deer.

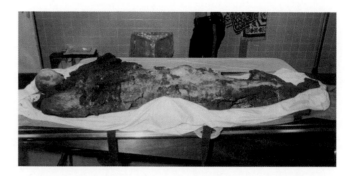

Forensic anthropology is the application of the science of physical anthropology to the legal process. The identification of skeletal, badly decomposed, or otherwise unidentified human remains is important for both legal and humanitarian reasons. The forensic anthropologist works closely with the medical examiner in the recovery and identification of the victim's remains. In addition to working up biological profiles of skeletal remains, the forensic anthropologist will assess the remains in a laboratory setting to determine the causes of any skeletal trauma. Often, the bones can reveal age, the medical history of the individual, DNA information, and the cause of death. *Morris County Sheriff's Office*

Behavioral analysts are often called in long after the crime has gone cold and the scene has been released, and they are often in psychologically upsetting territory. "We analyze the entire crime," said one agent. "The offender has left physical, as well as behavioral, clues." The technique is similar to a doctor evaluating a patient's symptoms to diagnose a condition. They take case reports, crime scene photos, witness statements, and autopsy reports, and attempt to re-create the scene mentally. They attempt to put themselves in the head of the offender—to think like he does, to sense his rage.

The physical evidence may sometimes provide connections; law enforcement can link different offenses at different times and places to one offender. The factual information taken from the crime scene is integrated with known psychological theory and the background of the victim to build a description of the offender or the most likely suspect based on age, race, gender, lifestyle, values, and if possible, criminal record.

Law enforcement has learned that the way a person acts in normal life is the way they will act in a crisis. Their behavior reflects their personality. If a person is obsessive compulsive or has other abnormal personality quirks, these will show up at the crime scene. A crime scene

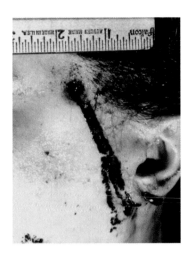

A bullet wound can be one of two types: a through and through (a wound with an entry wound and an exit wound) or an enclosed wound (where the bullet enters but does not exit, staying lodged in the body). The scale next to the entry wound is used to estimate the caliber of the bullet. The exact caliber will be determined at the autopsy. This may be a suicide, but the absence of gunshot residue near the wound and hands might rule out suicide and introduce homicide into the investigation. *Morris County Sheriff's Office*

"Local law enforcement or an FBI field office must request the participation of the Behavioral Analysis Unit," says Supervisory Special Agent Gerry Downes. "We don't just show up at a crime scene. Often, however, time is a critical factor. If local law enforcement calls us, we respond immediately but also let the FBI field office know. Our goal is to get involved in a support role from the get-go and help the local department focus their investigation."

investigator will look at other crime scenes for similar personality clues. Where they can link different offenses at different times and places to the same offender, investigators will attempt to determine the offender's next move and perhaps prevent another crime. Sometimes imagination is as important as knowledge. Behavioral analysis sometimes requires thinking out of the box.

"The process is like a three-legged stool," said one agent. "We use things we have learned during our education process, things we have learned through the research we do, and the things we have learned from other similar cases. We apply all of that to the case at hand and help get the local law enforcement pointed in the right direction. We do not arrest the individual; the local police do that."

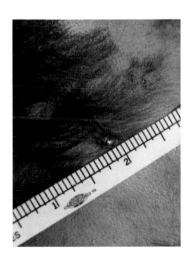

This bullet had the velocity to puncture but not exit the skull bone, but was still adequate to cause almost instantaneous death. Given desirable and reliable penetration, the only way to increase bullet effectiveness is to increase the severity of the wound by increasing the size of hole made by the bullet. The handgun is the primary weapon in law enforcement. It is the one weapon any officer or agent can be expected to have available whenever needed. Its purpose is to apply deadly force to not only protect the life of the officer and the lives of others, but to prevent serious physical harm to them as well. Reliable bullet fragmentation occurs in high-velocity projectile wounds (in excess of 2,000 feet per second) inflicted by soft or hollow-point bullets. Since the highest handgun velocities generally range from 1,400 to 1,500 feet per second at the muzzle, reliable fragmentation can only be achieved by constructing a hollow-point bullet that shatters inside the body. *Morris County Sheriff's Office*

## SIGNATURE ANALYSIS

Everyone acts in characteristic and often predictable ways. Some people are right-handed; others are left-handed. Everyone holds their pen a certain way. Some people use computers to write; others use a pen and notepad. Criminal behavior is also characteristic. How criminals act betrays them more often than what they say. The behavioral analysts look at a crime scene for the unique signature of the criminal. The offender's signature is the

> A ritual is an act unnecessary to the commission of the crime that is carried out in order to meet the emotional needs of the offender.

> Most serial offenders (88 percent) are white males in their twenties or thirties.

Crime scene investigators must dress in biohazard protective clothing. Refrigeration of human remains is necessary if the remains are not shipped immediately to the medical examiner. Decay takes place from the inside out and begins at death. Refrigeration will temporarily slow down the decay process. The removal of human remains is a careful process, as there may be additional evidence in or around the remains. Inside the refrigerated storage trailer, several bodies await postmortem examination. *FBI*

compulsive ritual behavior patterns that fulfill him emotionally. He may change his MO, but he cannot change his signature. It may be how he bound his victim, or marked her (bite marks, etc.), or arranged her body. It may be that he removes his victims' hearts, or in the case of the Alphabet Murders, he abducted and murdered at least three young Catholic schoolgirls who had the same initials. He cannot change this behavior.

"We look at what interaction occurred between the offender and the victim. If the victim is alive, he or she may be able to provide important clues from the offender's verbal behavior," said one investigator. "The offender may have a region-specific accent, frequently mispronounce certain words, or have a speech impediment."

> The Violent Criminal Apprehension Program (ViCAP) is a nationwide data information center designed to collect, collate, and analyze crimes of violence, specifically murder. The FBI provides the software to set up the ViCAP database to state and local law enforcement agencies free of charge.
>
> Cases examined by ViCAP include solved or unsolved homicides or attempts, especially those that involve an abduction, are apparently random, motiveless, or sexually oriented, or are known or suspected to be part of a series; missing persons, where the circumstances indicate a strong possibility of foul play and the victim is still missing; unidentified dead bodies, where the manner of death is known or suspected to be homicide; and sexual assault cases.
>
> Cases meeting the ViCAP submission criteria with an arrested or identified offender can be entered into the ViCAP system by law enforcement investigators for database comparison and possible matching with unsolved cases.

The clues the UNSUB leaves behind are individual to him. Did the offender cover the victim? That is a clue that he may have been close to the victim or at least knew her. They look at the time of day or night and the geography of the area. Did the crime occur in the suburbs, a wooded area, or an open field? All of these factors are important in developing a picture of the offender. What else may have occurred at the crime scene? Did the offender set a fire at each scene to destroy the evidence? If so, that is a possible clue to the individual's personality. He probably has low self-esteem and is socially incompetent. These clues are added to the offender's developing profile. Sometimes

A victim of a fire was unidentified, but investigators noticed a marking of some kind on the burned flesh on one arm. The medical examiner removed the flesh and proceeded to process the skin, which revealed a tattoo. The permanence and individuality of a tattoo makes it a valuable guide to identifying a person. *Morris County Sheriff's Office*

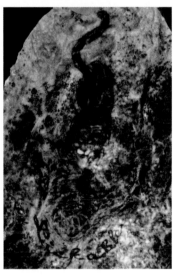

The flesh removed from the belly area revealed a black panther tattoo above the naval and the word "lickable" below it. These tattoos helped the investigators identify the victim. *Morris County Sheriff's Office*

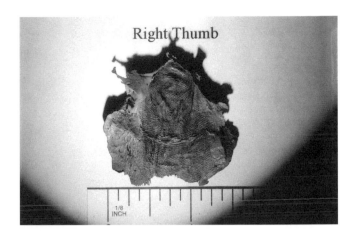

Right Thumb

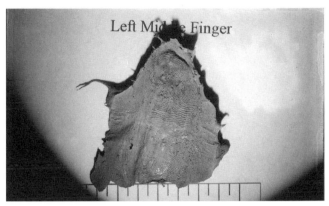

Left Middle Finger

In some cases, the remains do not reveal an adequate impression when the fingers are processed with the traditional ink and roll method. It is sometimes possible to acquire a good impression by using a special casting material. *Morris County Sheriff's Office*

the offender will use the bathroom or maybe wash blood off the weapon. Often the offender will take trophies from the victim, such as clothing, jewelry, or body parts, to re-create the fantasy and the satisfaction later that they derived from the crime. "There are also clues at the crime scene that cannot be collected, but are obvious: uncontrolled rage, overkill, fear and terror, for example," said one investigator. Since the crime may be cold, investigators may go back to the scene at the same time of day or night to attempt to see what the offender saw.

Behavioral links between crimes are a key component to identifying a serial offender. For example, one agency had three homicides in a six-month period, and they did not realize they were linked. "We have seen cases where the killer used a knife. He got full of the victim's blood and decided he was not going to do that again. He changes his

MO and decides to strangle his next victim. It takes a lot of work to strangle a person so he decides there has to be an easier way. These people learn," said one agent. "They learn the hard way, through experience, and they get better at what they do from one crime to the next."

They also learn from the media and from mistakes other serial offenders made that resulted in their apprehension. "Just because there are three homicides with three different methods does not mean they are not linked," one agent said. "If they are linked, the killer's signature will give us clues. The common denominator is usually the physical, sexual, and emotional nature of the crimes. After we look at the crime scene, the victim, and the rest of the data, we render an opinion as to whether it is or is not the same offender." Often the victim will provide valuable clues.

## VICTIMOLOGY

Victimology is an in-depth examination of the victim of a crime to learn more about the offender. Victimology may tell the investigator who the victim was, their health and personal history, social habits, and personality. It also may offer information on why they were chosen as a victim. In one case, it was simply because the victims were all between the ages of six and twelve, and had red hair.

The way an offender chooses a victim is important since it may give an insight into how the offender thinks, which affects how the offender acts. If the investigator is able to determine from the crime scene how the offender is acting now, he or she may be better able to determine the offender's future behavior.

A risk assessment will determine what, if anything, elevated an individual's potential for becoming the victim of a violent crime. Investigators will then place the victim on a risk continuum, from low to high. The lifestyle and the situational awareness of the victim, and the dynamics present at the time of the crime, are the primary focus in making this determination.

"When and where was the victim last seen alive?" asks the investigator. "The victim's lifestyle may be a factor that the offender takes into consideration." A bar-hopping individual who places classified ads for a companion in newspapers or on the Internet would put themselves at a higher risk. The street-corner prostitute would be much higher on the risk continuum than the high school student at home, who was at the low end of the risk continuum when she was abducted. It is soon obvious and reported right away when a high school student goes missing. The prostitute, by the very nature of her work, is transient, and it is often impossible to know when one goes missing until a body turns up. That may be one reason some killers choose that kind of victim; by the time the victim is discovered, the case is cold.

"We want to know everything there is to know about the victim. What was their personality like? Was the victim a fighter, or would they willingly go with somebody? The more we know about the victim, the more we can project about the offender," one investigator said. "If this guy grabs a female who puts up a fight, it tells us that he is willing to stick his neck out a lot further than he needs to. If there is evidence that the offender lingered with the body, had something to eat, for example, after the crime, then he is putting himself at extreme high risk, but it is part of his signature; it is something he has to do."

Body parts or skeletal remains discovered in remote areas may be the result of animal activity. A forensic anthropologist can determine the age, height, and sex of the victim by examining the skull, femur (thighbone), and pelvis of the victim. To determine gender, the forensic anthropologist will first look at the skull and hips. There are three points on the skull that give clues to gender—the ridge above the eyes, a bone below the ear, and the occiput, the bone at the lower back of the skull. The occiput and the bone below the ear are both muscle attachment sites and are more prominent in males. The hips are markedly narrower in males. With Forensic Discrimination (ForDisc) software, a forensic anthropologist can enter the skeletal measurements from an unknown crime victim, or even a partial skeleton (the length and diameter of a femur), and a computer program can accurately predict the race, sex, and stature of the person to whom the femur belonged.
*Morris County Sheriff's Office*

"A compliant victim tells us the offender may have planned the act and was watching the victim. He knows what she is like; she is vulnerable, and he knows he can easily do this because she will not put up a fight. The offender often plans his crime based on the victim's behavior," said one investigator.

## PSYCHOLOGICAL ASSESSMENT

Another method of examining a victim's life is a psychological assessment, most often performed by a forensic

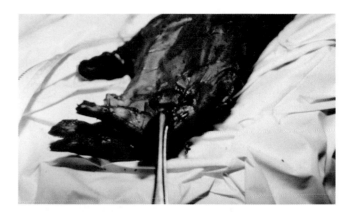

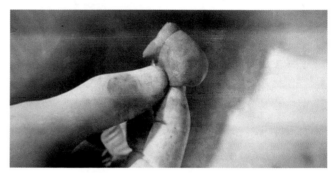

"In a fatal vehicle accident, we look for anything out of the ordinary. Is there an open cell phone on the floor? Is there a spilled cup of coffee? These may be signs that the driver was distracted," said one investigator. Motor vehicles in the wrong hands are as dangerous as loaded guns and are sometimes used with lethal intent in homicides. Investigators look at the scene for evidence about the speed and direction of the vehicle, visibility, and if the driver was applying the brakes. Once the scene has been processed, the vehicle is towed to a location where forensic investigators will look for mechanical failure or deliberate sabotage, such as cut brake lines. Computer software such as PC-Crash, a crash-modeling package, can re-create the accident. The investigator enters the information from the crash site, including length and radius of the tire marks on the road, the resting position of the vehicle, and type. The software then works regressively, using complex algorithms to calculate speed, direction, and more, before the impact. In the case of a homicide, this information may be presented in court. Suicide must be ruled out in a single vehicle fatality, and photographic evidence, such as how the victim's body is found, can be invaluable to investigators. With computer chips controlling many functions in a vehicle, investigators may look to altered or defective chips as contributing to a fatal accident. *Morris County Sheriff's Office*

This badly decomposed hand was not printable in its degraded condition. The medical examiner removed the skin from one finger and fit it over his gloved finger to obtain a readable print. *Morris County Sheriff's Office*

psychologist. It is a retrospective death evaluation, which attempts to discover the state of mind of the victim, preceding death.

If the death is equivocal—that is, one that can be interpreted in more than one way—investigators look for the classic warning signs of suicide: giving away possessions, or a sudden cheerfulness after a bout of depression. Wounds may provide clues. The victim has several shallow knife wounds in the chest area, called hesitation marks, and a knife imbedded in the heart. A basic question is could the victim have caused the wounds? Forensic psychologists will compile this information about the victim's psychological state, which will supplement the information provided by the medical examiner. Factors to consider include: What was the timeline of events leading up to the victim's death? Is there an alcohol or drug history? How did the victim deal with stress? Was there any recent stress in the victim's life?

If it is not a suicide, the information gathered may help with the investigation. The offender, in a sense, is the

A view of human remains found at a mass gravesite near Mosul, Iraq, during Operation Iraqi Freedom. The U.S. Army Criminal Investigation Command, along with Department of Defense forensic pathologists, is in Iraq investigating a mass grave crime scene to gather evidence for possible war crimes trials. *Defense Visual Information Center*

The differences between the organized and disorganized offender:

| Organized Offender | Disorganized Offender |
|---|---|
| Average to above-average intelligence | Below-average intelligence |
| Socially competent | Socially inadequate |
| Skilled work preferred | Unskilled work |
| Sexually competent | Sexually incompetent |
| High birth-order status | Low birth-order status |
| Father's work stable | Father's work unstable |
| Inconsistent childhood discipline | Harsh discipline as a child |
| Controlled mood during crime | Anxious mood during crime |
| Use of alcohol with crime | Minimal use of alcohol |
| Precipitating situational stress | Minimal situational stress |
| Living with partner | Living alone |
| Mobility with car in good condition | Lives/works near the crime scene |
| Follows crime in news media | Minimal interest in news media |
| May change jobs or leave town | Significant behavior change (e.g., drug or alcohol use) |

forensic psychologist's patient, and the victim is the medium the offender used to express his violence. Now the questions become: Did the victim have any old or current enemies, and what type of killer are we dealing with?

## ORGANIZED VERSUS DISORGANIZED SERIAL KILLERS

There are two broad categories of serial killers: organized and disorganized. Each has his own type of fantasy and leaves distinct personal characteristics at a crime scene that may later identify him. In some instances, these traits mix and cross over between each type.

The typical serial killer is organized and is the more sophisticated of the two. He is a sexual psychopath that usually premeditates his attack. These are crimes of anger, hostility, and control and power over the victim. The sexual assault is incidental. He may bring duct tape and rope to control his victim, and in one case a plastic container in which to restrain his victim and prevent the transfer of trace evidence. The organized offender may cut alarms or phone lines, and tape a window before breaking it. He is a true predator who will stalk his victim, say little, and gain control of him or her immediately. He may abduct his victim from one location, kill her at a second location, and dispose of the body at a third location. This offender may order his victim to bathe, or enter a lake, or discard the body in water in an attempt to eliminate trace evidence. The organized serial killer is generally sane, understands what he is doing, and shows no remorse. Organized serial killers are also smart enough and may manipulate a crime scene to make it look like it was the work of a disorganized offender.

The ham-fisted, or disorganized, offender is opportunistic and generally leaves much of himself at the crime scene—hairs, fibers, or DNA. His victim is often in the wrong place at the wrong time. He may have seen an opportunity to attack, surprised the victim, and, in a fit of rage, killed the victim. The weapon is also generally one of opportunity, such as a fireplace poker, and he will usually leave it at the crime scene. The disorganized offender will leave the scene in a jumbled condition, with the victim's possessions thrown about as a result of either a secondary crime, such as burglary, or the offender rummaging for a personal trophy of the victim. This type of offender generally has low interpersonal skills, does not have a great deal of knowledge about forensics, may have a mental disorder, and may be judged legally insane.

The serial offender left several behavioral clues in this case. It is clear he fits into the disorganized category. This was an inept attempt to burglarize the residence after his initial crime. The condition of the scene suggests the offender does not have past burglary convictions. An experienced burglar would also not leave his escape route littered with items that would hinder a quick exit.

## SERIAL KILLERS

Generally speaking, serial killers are defined by three or more kills, usually separated by a cooling-off period of days or years. Serial killers are feared by the public and sensationalized by the media. This publicity may lead to someone recognizing the killer, or it may influence the serial offender's behavior. It may make him more cautious, or it may embolden him to become more arrogant and reckless. This may ultimately lead to his capture, or could lead to more killing.

The homicidal troika of arson, late-stage bed-wetting, and cruelty to animals or other children are early signs of

Although it is a light impression of a footprint, it is also in a fragile condition. The running water may soon wash away important details. The print is photographed first, and then an impression is taken for possible match to a suspected piece of footwear. Prior to casting with Traxtone or other casting material, hair spray may be sprayed on the impression to stabilize it, and WD-40 may be sprayed into the impression to act as a release agent.

potential serial killers. The three most frequently reported behaviors included daydreaming, compulsive masturbation, and isolation. Serial killers may have been isolated, felt an inability to be social or socially accepted, and displayed a preoccupation with adolescent girls but awkwardness in establishing relationships with them. As children, they were sometimes abused, and as they grew up they committed petty crimes in defiance of authority. These crimes escalated into patterns of serious violent crimes by their mid- to late twenties.

> Among all homicide victims, women are particularly at risk for intimate killings, sex-related homicides, and murder by arson or poison. Among homicide offenders, women are generally more likely to commit murder as a result of an argument or murder by poison.

A serial offender may have experienced a precrime stressor in his personal life, such as a problem at school, work, home, or with law enforcement.

Serial killers generally begin their murderous careers close to home, in familiar neighborhoods, where they live or work, within the territorial boundaries called their

A U.S. Army soldier assigned to the U.S. Army Criminal Investigation Command (CID) removes a body from a mass grave crime scene. Note what appears to be a femur bone protruding from the cloth. *Defense Visual Information Center*

Discovery of these skeletal remains presumes a crime scene until an autopsy produces a cause of death. The crime scene team will have to figure out who the person was and what happened. If a body is abandoned long enough, the animals may scatter the remains, and what is left may be unrecognizable. *Morris County Sheriff's Office*

comfort zone. It is a place where they can be identified, but it is also a place that provides a known escape route.

Serial killers begin traveling out of their comfort zone when media attention begins to make them feel empowered, or by circumstances beyond their control—for example, if the killer is a military person who is transferred frequently. Ultimately, it is virtually impossible to detect a serial killer before the fact, since many seem to be normal in their everyday lives. They are usually white males, with above-average intelligence, clean-cut, the typical boy-next-door type.

## CHILD ABDUCTION

The worst of the serial killers prey on the most vulnerable of society, innocent children. Authorities cannot agree on the number of children that go missing every year, or on what becomes of them. In abduction cases, in the first twenty-four to thirty-six hours, if the victim is not found alive, the case generally does not have a favorable outcome.

Kidnapping is the abducting of a person of any age against his/her will, or from the control of a parent or guardian, from one place to another. The person taken does not have freedom of movement, will, or decision through violence, force, threat, or intimidation. All kidnapping is a criminal felony, and the offender's capture usually involves some related criminal act, such as holding the person for ransom, sexual and/or sadistic abuse, or rape. It includes abducting the person due to irresistible impulse and a parent taking and hiding a child in violation of court order. An included crime is false imprisonment. Any harm to the victim coupled with kidnapping can raise the degree of felony for the injury, and can result in a capital, or death, penalty.

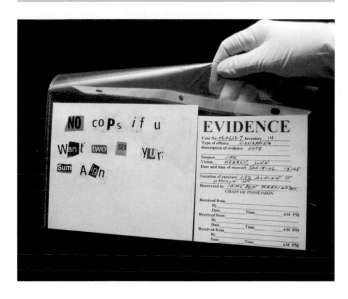

A pieced-together threat note is generally not from a stranger, and the offender reveals a great deal to the crime scene investigator. In threat letters, about 1 percent of the offenders put together notes like this. The offender uses the pieced-together note to hide his identity since the victim would likely recognize the handwriting. When a threat note uses cut-out letters, it is generally not from a stranger, but from someone who has an emotional attachment of some sort to the victim.

In the case of child abduction, the FBI uses a child abduction response plan, a crime-specific manual for the on-scene investigators. It lists things that should be done, such as an initial search of the entire house,

including a crime scene search of the child's room for fibers, hair, and DNA samples. "It is basic police work at this point," said one agent, "but if you miss anything, bad things can happen. For instance, there have been cases where children accidentally suffocated near the home and weren't located for several days."

"One of the first things you do in a child abduction case is interview the family. The parents should be interviewed separately," said another agent. "If a child goes missing, there is often a chance one parent is involved. Some tough questions that need to be asked: 'Is your child involved with drugs or alcohol? Has he or she exhibited any violent behavior lately, or is he or she sexually active?' We try to eliminate the family members as suspects." The family should undergo a polygraph test as part of the elimination. "If one of them agrees to a polygraph and then they start backing up," one agent said, "well then, we may have a clue there."

The next important step is the neighborhood canvass. Canvassing the neighborhood is an attempt to seek witnesses who may not know they have useful information about the crime. If the canvass is done properly, it will usually lead to an early resolution. "You're going to come up with a witness who saw something," said one investigator. "Perhaps someone

According to the FBI, child abduction and serial homicide are considered two of the most serious violent crime problems facing the United States. Homicide is the second leading cause of death for persons fifteen to twenty-four years of age and the leading cause of death for African Americans in this age group.

related to the offender. Nine times out of ten, when there is an unsuccessful outcome, the neighborhood canvass is not done properly," he said.

In the neighborhood canvass, every person, in every house, should be interviewed, because every person sees different things. That includes children. They see things too. "We provide a neighborhood canvass form of twenty-five to thirty questions," said one FBI agent. "It takes a long time to do it properly. If the local law enforcement uses the same form, they will ask the questions the same way and we will get more consistent results."

## COLD CASES SOLVED

To catch killers, FBI behavioral analysts often probe the dark side of the human psyche and get inside the mind of a killer. In September 1996, in Spotsylvania, Virginia, young Sophia Silva returned home from school, grabbed a soda, and walked outside to sit on the porch to do her homework. From a behavioral point of view, she was at low risk to become a victim. Within minutes, she was gone, abducted in broad daylight. Her murdered body was found in a creek one month later. Her body had been bound with rope, and the killer used dozens of knots on the rope. There was trace evidence of the killer on the victim.

Eight months later the killer struck again. In May 1997, the school bus dropped fifteen-year-old Kristin and twelve-year-old Kati Lisk off at their home. When the girls' parents returned home from work one hour later, the two sisters were missing. Five days later, their bodies were found floating in a river, presumably sexually assaulted and murdered.

Unsolved homicide cases are never closed but can go cold if enough evidence cannot be found to identify or convict an offender.

The police department in Spring Hill, Texas, requested a helicopter to perform an aerial survey and photograph the scene of a suspected serial killing. The police officer on the left photographs the latest crime scene. Often, a bird's-eye view and later development of the film will reveal clues or evidence not easily seen from the ground.

The crime lab discovered that trace evidence found on Sophia Silva's body matched trace evidence found on the bodies of the Lisk sisters. One person was responsible for all three murders. The FBI compared the genetic profiles of the four hundred thousand felons in the Combined DNA Index System (CODIS) database at the time from forty-six states with evidence in the unsolved Silva–Lisk slayings. There were no matches.

Five years went by without a break in any of the cases. "We wondered," said an FBI analyst, "if the killer was dead or in jail." Experts speculate on what happens when the killer stops killing. Some may commit suicide, die in accidents or of natural causes, become incarcerated, or relocate to another area.

The Combined DNA Index System (CODIS) program provides software and support services to enable state and local crime laboratories to establish databases of convicted offenders, unsolved crime scenes, and missing persons. CODIS allows these forensic laboratories to exchange and compare DNA profiles electronically, thereby linking serial violent crimes, especially sexual assaults, to one another, and to identify suspects by matching DNA from crime scenes to convicted offenders.

CODIS has recorded more than five hundred matches linking serial violent crimes to one another or identifying suspects by matching crime scene evidence to known convicted offenders. These matches have aided more than one thousand violent crime investigations. CODIS is cross-referenced every Friday in an attempt to match old cases with new DNA inputs.

National Missing Persons DNA Database Program personnel develop DNA profiles from reference samples of biological relatives of missing persons and unidentified human remains. Mitochondrial DNA (mtDNA) profiles are developed from the samples and, when feasible, nuclear DNA analysis is performed. The database stores the DNA profiles in CODIS, which allows laboratories in the system to share DNA information relating to missing persons. The database assists in identifying missing persons on a national level.

The FBI later learned that the killer met an eighteen-year-old woman who fulfilled the fantasies he had sought in his kidnapped victims. When she reached the age of twenty-three, she became too old for him, and he went seeking his fourth victim.

In June 2002, the killer struck again. In a small town in South Carolina, a man posing as a magazine salesman approached a fifteen-year-old girl watering her garden. He pulled a gun and forced her into his car. Investigators later decided he probably kidnapped Sophia Silva and the Lisk girls the same way. He drove his victim to his apartment, tied her up, and raped her. Later that night, the offender fell asleep in another room. When the girl heard him snoring, she freed herself from the ropes and escaped from the apartment; she was spotted running naked in a parking lot, still wearing handcuffs. The motorist called the police. When the man woke up and saw his teenage victim gone, he methodically packed his car and drove off. However, police had a physical description and a tip that he was heading to Florida. When the police cornered him near Sarasota, he pulled a gun and shot himself to death.

Police learned the killer's name was Richard Mark Evonitz. When police searched his apartment, they found newspaper clippings describing the Lisk sisters' abduction. Evonitz's hair was found on all three bodies, and Evonitz's car had Kristin Lisk's palm print. After five years, the killer of Sophia Silva and Kristin and Kati Lisk

had been found. His fourth intended victim, the brave teenager who was able to survive, helped solve the case.

Evonitz is dead, but the search for more of his victims goes on. Authorities believe Evonitz struck often over the years. He has been identified in two criminal acts in Florida, and authorities are currently looking back at the many places he lived over the years for more victims who fit his MO.

## CODIS-LINKED SERIAL RAPISTS

As the Combined DNA Index System (CODIS) continues to be populated with convicted offenders' DNA, it is proving to be a valuable forensic tool for law enforcement. In 1986, a college professor in Flint, Michigan, was brutally raped and murdered in her home. An AFIS search of the Michigan State Police files was negative, so no suspects developed in this crime. In 1991, a flight attendant was raped and murdered in Romulus, Michigan. Again, there were no suspects. In 2001, DNA from the 1986 offense was input into CODIS. It matched the 1991 offense. The Flint Michigan Police Department's cold case squad submitted three latent fingerprints from the 1986 homicide to the FBI's IAFIS. One of the latent fingerprints was identified with a suspect. The suspect had no arrest record in Michigan. The police wanted more proof, so they did not immediately arrest the suspect. Instead, they followed him and retrieved a napkin he used in a restaurant. DNA from the napkin

Hypodermic injection of tissue builders such as Hydrol, a viscous gel, into this fake hand is a way of practicing the process for forensic tissue rehydryation and finger ridge enhancement. Similar fluids, when injected into supporting soft tissues, will often overcome the problem of crevices and wrinkles in decaying flesh. *Morris County Sheriff's Office*

Using CODIS, the Illinois State Police Laboratory linked a 1999 solved sexual assault case to three other sexual assaults in which the suspect was previously unknown. The 1999 case involved a sexual assault on two female college students who were unable to identify the offender. Police, however, were able to develop a suspect from witnesses' descriptions and circumstantial evidence. CODIS matched this suspect's DNA profile to three other cases that occurred in 1994 and 1995.

matched DNA from both homicides. He was arrested and charged with both crimes.

In October 1999, Alan Lee Hoff was arrested and charged with two burglaries in Kissimmee, Florida. A few days later, a fingerprint check identified Hoff as Claude Dean Hull, wanted for burglary and sexual assault in

Arizona and California. Hull, who also used other aliases, was first arrested in California in 1991 for rape at gunpoint in Clovis, and two rapes in Fresno. He fled California to avoid prosecution.

On August 23, 1995, a nineteen-year-old female was sexually assaulted in Phoenix, Arizona. The Phoenix crime laboratory developed a DNA profile and searched the Arizona State DNA database. The search disclosed a DNA match to Claude Hull's profile.

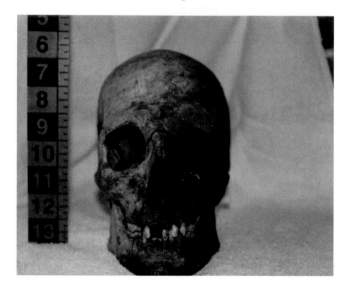

While the skull can reveal age, race, and gender, lab technicians, using special electronic facial recognition software, can produce two- and three-dimensional facial reconstruction from skeletal remains, facial age progressions, and postmortem reconstructions. A technician using modeling clay can produce a three-dimensional form from the computer image or build out the skeletal remains. *FBI*

Forensic odontology is the subdiscipline of dentistry that applies the principles of dental science to legal issues. Dental remains are important to the identification process because they offer the best means of positive identification of a skeleton or unrecognizable individual; they are durable and may contain surviving mtDNA. There are several reasons why the dentition is especially valuable for human identification. Tooth enamel is the hardest substance in the human body, which makes teeth strong and capable of surviving in conditions that are particularly harmful to other human tissues. An individual's dental records are often the best means of identification due to the unique characteristics that are available from teeth, including growth patterns and commonly observed dental treatments, such as extraction, fillings, crowns, and partial dentures. The dental records from an individual, if available, are compared with the remains by the forensic odontologists. Ideally, the forensic odontologist will have antemortem (before death) X-rays to use for comparison, but even handwritten charts and treatment notes can be critical to the identification process. *Morris County Sheriff's Office*

In 1998, two women in Phoenix and one in Scottsdale, Arizona, were raped by a man using the same MO as Claude Dean Hull. DNA profiles from these crime scenes were entered into CODIS and matched Hull's DNA profile.

Florida police arrested Hull in 1999, and he confessed to one count of rape and three counts of burglary in Florida. He also confessed to raping women in Arizona and California, as well as committing numerous burglaries, forgery, and auto theft. He was sentenced to fifty-five years in a Florida prison.

On March 23, 2001, after pleading guilty to four counts of sexual assault, one count of attempted sexual assault, and one count of attempted sexual assault of a minor, serial rapist Claude Dean Hull was sentenced to

At this crime scene, the person committed suicide with the shotgun resting on his right arm. The pellets from the shotgun shell struck the person with such force that blood was projected at great speed, spraying out in tiny droplets on the wall. The crime scene investigator will take overall photos, specific location shots, body shots (prior to moving), and specific shots of wounds. Crime scene cleanup is a necessary part of the process. The companies that do this work generally do not have to advertise. Business referrals come from the Internet, police, paramedics, and coroners. A typical job takes a team of three technicians in biohazard suits about eight hours and may cost $3,000 or more. Most often, anything touched by blood must be physically removed from the building and destroyed, such as flooring and walls. *Morris County Sheriff's Office*

fifty-six years in an Arizona prison, to be served after the completion of his Florida sentence.

In 1978, an individual went on trial for a knife-point sexual assault in Manhattan, but it ended with no verdict. Facing retrial, the accused fled the state. However, a piece of physical evidence remained in a file—underwear from the crime scene.

In 2004, when the individual went to buy a gun in Georgia, a background check turned up a warrant on him for the 1973 New York rape. By then, DNA analysis was in the mainstream, and the physical evidence from the 1973 rape case was in CODIS.

Law enforcement connected the DNA from the New York rape to a series of unsolved sexual assaults in Maryland and New Jersey, between 1987 and 1993. The

The body of one of serial killer Richard Mark Evonitz's victims is removed from the crime scene. The more the killer handled the victim, the greater the chance he left some of his DNA. However, in this case, Evonitz's DNA was not in the CODIS database. He was off the FBI's radar for five years, and they wondered if he was dead or in jail. *FBI*

All FBI underwater search and evidence response team (USERT) diver candidates must be special agents and possess an open-water diving certification with five to ten dives completed. They are selected from a limited group of special agent open-water divers who first have to pass medical exams, stressing fitness as divers, and then participate in a series of rigorous aquatic tests just to qualify as candidates for advanced training. They are highly trained to conduct investigations in any aquatic environment and are experienced in search and recovery of human remains and evidentiary material from bodies of water under the worst diving conditions imaginable. Because most diving conditions are zero visibility, USERT divers are trained to search the bottom literally blindfolded. *FBI*

All death scenes must be thoroughly documented. Side one of a death scene case study form deals in very specific details about the death scene area, the remains, various temperatures at the scene, and weather observations. *Morris County Sheriff's Office*

Side two of the form deals with insect activity on and around the body. Morris County Sheriff's Office

forensic evidence linked nine rapes near Silver Spring, Maryland, to the suspect, possibly seven more in that area, plus two assaults in Morris County, New Jersey, and two in New York City.

## INTERVIEWING A SUSPECT

Capturing a suspected serial offender is not always the end of the case. Obtaining a confession may be as difficult as finding the suspect. Through carefully structured interviews, a crime scene investigator can learn about the subject's needs, fears, concerns, attitudes, or the emotional trigger that will cause him to talk. Behavioral analysts will advise local law enforcement on how to confront their suspect during the interview. They may suggest how to evaluate the suspect's demeanor (i.e., the use of their words and gestures), and what interview techniques to use—the soft or hard approach (good cop, bad cop), or appeal to his ego—and what would probably be the best time to conduct the interview, late at night or early in the morning when we are all the most vulnerable.

## LOOKING FOR DECEPTION

"When you lie," said one investigator, "you have to remember the truth and the lies." Criminals lie, and it is up to the investigators to recognize deception, distortion, exaggeration, and lying. Sweating, dilated pupils, hand or lip tremors, facial tics, and failure to make eye contact can often give away more information than the person being interviewed intends to reveal.

"Lying requires the individual to keep facts straight, yet make the story believable enough to withstand close examination," said one investigator. Usually, one lie requires backup with another lie. The untruthful person

U.S. Customs and Border Protection officers encountered an individual from Jamaica who had his fingerprints and footprints replaced with someone else's. The surgery appears to have been poorly done. Fingerprints develop in a fetus at about thirteen weeks and remain the same throughout a person's life. Minor cuts, scrapes, and burns can temporarily affect the ridge patterns, but the original pattern is repeated on the newly healed skin. More serious injuries that reach the deeper layer of the skin, the dermis, can damage the cells that promote skin growth and leave a scar. Still, an identity could be established from the nonscarred areas, as well as from a person's palms and footprints. *Morris County Sheriff's Office*

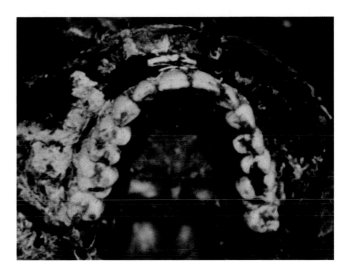

The remains of this individual are unrecognizable, but the dentition is in place for a forensic odontologist to chart the teeth, and if a comparison record is available, a positive identification of the individual can be made. *Morris County Sheriff's Office*

## LINEUP

Identification of suspects through mug shots, lineups, grainy photographs, and composite sketches at times may be problematic for police, and relying on eyewitness accounts alone may lead to wrongful convictions. Although these methods are still used, court challenges have encouraged police to concentrate on solid forensic evidence.

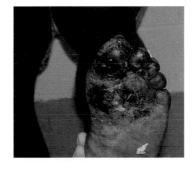

The individual's feet show altered toe prints and alterations on the ball of the foot. What is also evident is the possibility of early gangrene setting in. *Morris County Sheriff's Office*

Serial homicides catch the public and media's attention and provoke inexplicable explanations for why they happen. Between 1982 and 1984, the Green River Killer murdered forty-nine people but was never caught, although there was a suspect. The suspect died of a heart attack, and after his death, the killings stopped. Between January and August 1982, forty-eight patients in a Midwest veteran's hospital died mysteriously. Between 1987 and 1995, eight homosexual men were stabbed to death in the Chesapeake, Virginia, area. Between 1990 and 1997 in the Richmond, Virginia, area, the Golden Years Killer invaded the homes of twenty-four women between the ages of fifty-five and ninety, and assaulted and murdered them.

In 1974, Theodore Robert Bundy killed eighteen women. His total for that year may be higher. It is not lower. He collected victims in Washington, Utah, and Colorado. His preferred methods of execution were strangulation and bludgeoning. After his arrest, Bundy acknowledged stalking and killing from 1971, when he was twenty-four, to 1973. There is speculation that his career in murder began earlier than that, perhaps while he was still in his teens. Bundy confessed to over thirty murders. In 1978, Bundy claimed six Florida victims, five of them on one night. A reasonable estimate of the totals, factoring in his time in jail, suggests forty to fifty victims over eight years.

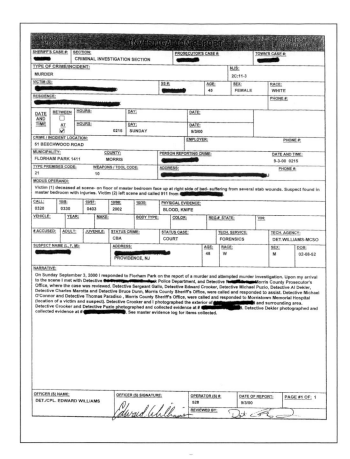

Final homicide report. *Morris County Sheriff's Office*

Side two

prefers concealing the truth rather than making up a fictitious story. The liar will convey the truth up to the event he wants to hide.

"We routinely look for nonverbal signals to determine if a person is not being truthful," said one investigator. "Left-handed people usually look to the left when lying. A right-handed person looking to the left may be searching his memory for the truthful answer. If he looks right, he is trying to create information, or lie," said one investigator. People who attempt to conceal information often breathe faster, taking a series of short breaths, followed by one long, deep breath.

There are seven biologically built-in emotional expressions on the face: joy, anger, sadness, disgust, fear, surprise, and contentment. To a trained investigator, these emotions reflect on the suspect's face and provide valuable insight to the person, how they feel, their current state of mind, and their attitudes toward others, to name a few.

By mirroring a suspect's nonverbal behavior, his mannerisms, the way he sits, or matching the manner in which they say something or their choice of words, investigators can increase rapport and enhance communication. As a result, the potential for gaining crucial information needed to help resolve investigations improves significantly. "Once interviewers establish rapport, barriers disappear, trust grows, and an exchange of information follows," said one investigator.

## CONCLUSION

More than 100 years after Sherlock Holmes began solving crimes, forensic science can brag of abilities that once were magical and unrealistic, even to the logical and well-reasoned Holmes. Crime scene investigators have powerful tools at their disposal, from DNA fingerprinting, microanalytic instrumentation, sophisticated chemical analysis, and the results of years of psychological studies on why

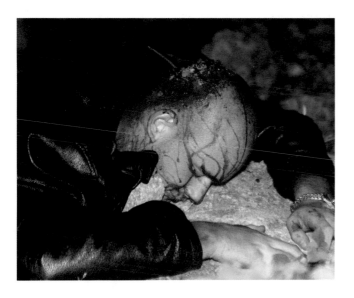

Some crime scene and first responder training involves simulations. This is a simulated fatal trauma to the head. Through this type of training, attempts are made to develop an attitude that will allow the individual to more quickly deal with real trauma. *Defense Visual Information Center*

Forensic hypnosis is used to enhance or probe the memory or recall of an individual for information in a criminal case. Forensic hypnosis places a person in a trancelike state that may resemble sleep but is instead an altered state of consciousness more akin to a lucid dream. While the individual is in a trance, he or she is alert but focused in a way that differs from the normal conscious state.

In 1941, AT&T's Bell Laboratories developed voice spectrograms as a means of identifying suspects from characteristics of their speech.

people commit crimes. They have the ability to revisit horrendous crimes to learn how to prevent them in the future, and they routinely provide expert witness testimony in courts of law. Crime scene investigation has come a long way since the days of Sherlock Holmes, and every day, new technologies are being developed, benefiting crime scene investigators in their quest to discover the truth.

The FBI's Uniform Crime Reports show that, in 2004, 89 percent of murder victims were age eighteen or older. Of all murder victims, 45 percent were twenty to thirty-four years old. By gender, males comprised 82.2 percent of arrestees for violent crime. Black males eighteen to twenty-four years old have the highest homicide victimization rates. Their rates are more than double the rates for black males age twenty-five and older, and four times the rates for black males fourteen to seventeen years old.

In August 1987, thirteen-year-old Jessica Standridge's parents reported her missing. Local law enforcement searched but did not find the victim. Skeletal remains were located in June 1988. In 1993, a private company attempted to perform DNA testing on the skeletal remains, but the tests were inconclusive. In September 2002, the National Missing Persons DNA Database Program performed mtDNA analysis on a tooth from the recovered skull and on a reference sample obtained from the missing girl's mother. The mtDNA profile of the tooth was the same as the mtDNA profile from the mother's reference sample. This information allowed the police to redirect the focus of their investigation.

Some criminals leave obvious evidence behind. A map marking a possible escape route was found at the scene of the crime.

In 1985, a fourteen-year-old girl was raped and murdered. Crime scene investigators here re-created the scene for a documentary being made on the violent crime. The depression in the ground is the actual spot where the girl's body was found. The individual without a hat is retired Detective Sergeant George Duechar, the lead crime scene investigator on the crime. The victim was stabbed twenty-seven times "in ritualistic fashion," according to the medical examiner. Detectives saw the crime as one of opportunity and not one committed by an organized or serial offender. The nineteen-year-old offender was apprehended, tried, and convicted of murder, kidnapping, and sexual assault, and is serving 150 years.

Small pieces of evidence at a crime scene are sometimes difficult to see, given the amount of leaves on the ground. That is why it is important to clearly mark it and photograph it.

Since the introduction of digital cameras, crime scene investigators can get instant feedback on the photos they make. Detective James Rae is reviewing some photos to determine if they present the scene properly. Detective Corporal Bill Stitt is in the background.

# Glossary

**AAFS:** American Academy of Forensic Sciences

**AFIS:** Automated Fingerprint Identification System

**Apneic:** victim has no pulse or respiration

**CID:** criminal investigation command

**CIS:** criminal investigation section

**CJIS:** Criminal Justice Information System

**CODIS:** Combined DNA Index System

**CSI:** crime scene investigator

**DOJ:** Department of Justice

**FDLE:** Federal Department of Law Enforcement

**Det.:** detective

**DNA:** deoxyribonucleic acid

**DOA:** dead on arrival

**FITT:** frequency, intensity, time, and type

**ERT:** evidence response technician, evidence response team, emergency response team

**FBI:** Federal Bureau of Investigation

**GEA:** groove engraved area

**GRC:** general rifling characteristics

**GSR:** gunshot residue

**HMRT:** hazardous materials response team

**IAFIS:** Integrated Automated Fingerprint Identification System

**LEA:** land engraved area

**LECR:** law enforcement candidate record

**MCSO:** Morris County Sheriff's Office

**MO:** *modus operandi* (method of operation)

**mtDNA:** mitochondrial DNA

**NBC:** nuclear, biological, or chemical

**NCJOSI:** National Criminal Justice Officer Selection Inventory

**NCIC 2000:** National Crime Information Center

**nDNA:** nuclear DNA

**NIBIN:** National Integrated Ballistic Information Network

**NTSB:** National Transportation Safety Board

**Plt.:** patrolman

**POE:** point of entry

**PPO:** probationary police officer

**POWER:** Peace Officer Wellness Evaluation Report

**RUVIS:** Reflected Ultra-Violet Imaging Systems

**SO:** sheriff's office

**SOP:** standard operating procedure

**STO:** supervising training officer

**SWAT:** special weapons and tactics

**UNSUB:** unknown subject

**USERT:** underwater search and evidence response team

**ViCAP:** Violent Criminal Apprehension Program

**WMD:** weapons of mass destruction

# Index

**To Be an FBI Special Agent**
ISBN 0-7603-2118-3

**To Be a U.S. Naval Aviator**
ISBN 0-7603-2163-9

**To Be a U.S. Air Force Pilot**
ISBN 0-7603-1791-7

**To Be a U.S. Secret Service Agent**
ISBN 0-7603-2293-7

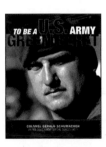

**To Be a U.S. Army Green Beret**
ISBN 0-7603-2107-8

**To Be a U.S. Army Ranger**
ISBN 0-7603-1314-8

**To Be a U.S. Marine**
ISBN 0-7603-1788-7

**The Spycraft Manual: The Insider's Guide to Espionage Techniques**
ISBN 0-7603-2074-8

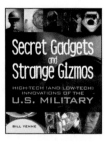

**Secret Gadgets and Strange Gizmos: High-Tech (and Low-Tech) Innovations of the U.S. Military**
ISBN 0-7603-2115-9